THE REFERENCE SHELF   VOLUME 35 NUMBER 4

REPRESENTATIVE AMERICAN SPEECHES: 1962-1963

EDITED BY LESTER THONSSEN

Professor of Speech, The City College of New York

THE H. W. WILSON COMPANY
NEW YORK   1963

THE REFERENCE SHELF

The books in this series reprint articles, excerpts from books, and addresses on current issues, social trends, and other aspects of American life, and occasional surveys of foreign countries. There are six separately bound numbers in each volume, all of which are generally published in the same calendar year. One number is a collection of recent speeches on a variety of subjects; each of the remaining numbers is devoted to a single subject and gives background information and discussion from varying points of view, followed by a comprehensive bibliography.

Subscribers to the current volume receive the books as issued. The subscription rate is $12 ($15 foreign) for a volume of six numbers. The price of single numbers is $3 each.

PRINTED IN THE UNITED STATES OF AMERICA

22469

PREFACE

Since antiquity, critics have written about the decline of oratory. The theme is persistent and evidently attractive. But somehow public speaking lives on, indeed gains strength. Amazed perhaps at the resilience of the art, some modern prophets have changed their attack. Instead of repeating the cliché "Oratory is dead," they harp upon its futility. According to them, nobody pays any attention to the spoken word. On the face of it, such a remark is nonsense. True, many media today compete for attention in persuasion and instruction. But if no one takes the spoken word seriously, why do politicians think increasingly well of television debates? Why do politically wise candidates still regard face-to-face speaking as indispensable to effective campaigning? Why do leaders in industry, the professions, and public service rely heavily upon personal appearance and oral expression rather than upon printed leaflets only, when instruction and persuasion are their objectives? And why do administrators at all levels of authority spend time, as they do occasionally, restraining or curbing oral communication? Evidently what is spoken makes a difference, a significant difference, even though the same material may be easy to come by in print.

Speaking and writing continue to play complementary roles; neither is in decay, both are influential. Their interplay will continue for, as the Most Reverend A. M. Ramsey, Archbishop of Canterbury, said in a presidential address to the English Association in 1960, "words are made and enjoyed by voice and ear and eye together, and none of the three will resign its role so long as the use of words remains."

This is not to overlook the difference between spoken and written discourse. In lifeless print an originally effective speech may appear dull, uninspired. Clearly, a speech suffers in the process of translation from words heard to words read. It loses something, its distinguishing mark—the authentic sign of the living speaker. "Most speeches, when recalled," said Lord Birkett, the distinguished advocate and judge who died in early 1962, "are without the fire and the glow with which they were invested by the speaker's presence; the dramatic setting has gone; and the emotions of the moment have vanished irrevocably." No amount of historical analysis can faithfully reconstruct the full context in which the speech had a *real* existence. I believe, however, that the speeches selected for inclusion in this twenty-sixth edition reveal something of what the Archbishop of Canterbury called "the eye's appreciation of words on paper as well as the ear's response to them when spoken."

Whether or not all of these addresses had or will have appreciable influence on public life, no one can say precisely. But they expressed important facts of observation and conscience. Because they dealt with ideas—some old, some new—that are of lasting concern to every American, they received thoughtful attention.

I trust that students will find certain ideas or convictions expressed in these speeches sufficiently provocative to stimulate independent analysis and inquiry. The thoughts and imaginative thrusts of the young are as necessary as those of the more experienced in assessing the aspirations, frustrations, and perplexities in our day.

As in previous years, public officials and private citizens have generously supplied copies of speeches for my examination. I am of course grateful to the persons represented in this edition for permission to reprint their addresses. For counsel and assistance at various stages in the preparation of this volume, I am indebted to John Jamieson, Margaret P. Edge, and Ruth Ulman of The H. W. Wilson Company, Margaret Robb of the University of Colorado, Ota Thomas Reynolds of Hunter College of the City University of New York, David H. Russell and Elizabeth Fatherson Russell of the University of California at Berkeley, C. W. Reynolds, Dorothea Thonssen, and Magdalene Kramer of Teachers College, Columbia University.

LESTER THONSSEN

New York City
July 1963

CONTENTS

BOLD WORDS AND DECISIVE ACTION

AN ADDRESS TO THE NATION [1]

JOHN F. KENNEDY [2]

Twenty-five years ago, Franklin D. Roosevelt called for world support to stem Japan's aggression in China. Likening international lawlessness to an epidemic of physical illness, he urged the peace-loving nations to join in a quarantine "to protect the health of the community against the spread of the disease." War is a contagion, he said, and "we are adopting such measures as will minimize our risk of involvement, but we cannot have complete protection in a world of disorder in which confidence and security have broken down."

The world condition on October 5, 1937—the date of Roosevelt's talk in Chicago—was sharply different from that of our day. But the ultimate issue was the same: the achievement of a stable peace for all mankind. Little wonder, then, that those who remember pre-World War II days thought back to Roosevelt's words when they heard President Kennedy's radio-television address of October 22, 1962, in which he announced the placing of a quarantine on all shipments of offensive military materials to Cuba.

Other parallels with the Kennedy speech have been mentioned. When Woodrow Wilson called for a declaration of war against Germany on April 2, 1917, he too spoke of a choice that the United States could not make: "We will not choose the path of submission and suffer the most sacred rights of our nation and our people to be ignored or violated. The wrongs against which we now array ourselves are no common wrongs; they cut to the very roots of human life." Franklin D. Roosevelt's speech of December 8, 1941, after the attack on Pearl Harbor, voiced a similar conviction. Winston Churchill's address before the House of Commons on October 5, 1938, warning the British to face up to the realities of the Nazi threat, also comes to mind, although this was observation after an act of appeasement at Munich.

Describing the nature and extent of the secret military build-up in Cuba, President Kennedy resolved not to permit an outside power to establish a nuclear arsenal in the Caribbean: "Our unswerving objec-

[1] Text furnished by Pierre Salinger, press secretary to the President, with permission for this reprint.

[2] For biographical note, see Appendix.

tive . . . must be to prevent the use of these missiles against this or any other country, and to secure their withdrawal or elimination from the Western Hemisphere." Voicing a conviction not unfamiliar to many who heard Franklin D. Roosevelt, President Kennedy declared that "the 1930's taught us a clear lesson: Aggressive conduct, if allowed to go unchecked and unchallenged, ultimately leads to war."

An anxious world, hoping for the best but expecting much less, watched the swift happenings during the following week. According to John Pringle, writing in the *Listener* (London), when the President came to the words " 'I have directed the following initial steps . . . ,' one could almost hear humanity holding its breath. No Caesar ever crossed his Rubicons—dragging the rest of us with him—quite so publicly."

At ten o'clock on October 23 the blockade began, and with it the fear of a confrontation between a Soviet vessel and an American naval unit. On the same day the Organization of American States, by a vote of 19 to 0 with one abstention, demonstrated its unity by authorizing the use of armed force, if necessary, to settle the crisis. An emergency session of the Security Council of the United Nations immediately entered upon a debate on the issue. After three days of sharp controversy, particularly between Ambassador Adlai E. Stevenson, the United States representative, and Valerian A. Zorin, the Soviet representative, the United States and the Soviet Union agreed to engage in private talks with U Thant, then Acting Secretary General of the United Nations, on ways to resolve the conflict and spare the world from possible thermonuclear destruction. Mankind moved back from the edge of the chair on Sunday, October 28, when President Kennedy and Premier Khrushchev agreed tentatively on a plan to end the emergency. The Soviet Union would dismantle the offensive weapons and ship them home. The United States would lift the quarantine following appropriate observation of the dismantling, after which she would offer a pledge not to invade Cuba.

"Now that the two super-powers have faced the brink and warily drawn back from the abyss," commented the New York *Times* editorially, "this decision offers hope not only for a solution of the Cuban crisis but also of the broader problems dividing East and West." Admitting that "the vision is almost too idyllic to be real," the editor nonetheless concluded that "it injects new vigor and hope into the pursuit of a peace of benefit to all mankind."

President Kennedy's speech dominated the news to the virtual exclusion of many other major events, including the Chinese-Indian clash and the political campaigns at home. It is comforting to know, however, that even in the darkest moments man usually sees a bit of light. While concentrating on his serious business, he confidently attends to matters of less cosmic concern. Reportedly the Navy, while conducting the blockade, took time to award cash and a paid vacation in the mountains to a Marine for his recipe for Navy bean soup.

The address of October 22 was not the sort to which one gives a respectful hearing in the evening, only to forget it at the start of a new day. It was not an inspirational call for support of a proposal; it was a solemn, firm announcement of a decision already made and ready for execution. It may well rank as one of the major documents of our time.

With minor exceptions, the response was impressively favorable. Within three days after the delivery of the speech, some fifty thousand telegrams had arrived at the White House. According to Press Secretary Pierre Salinger, the ratio in favor of the presidential decision ran about 22 to 1.

This Government, as promised, has maintained the closest surveillance of the Soviet military build-up on the island of Cuba. Within the past week, unmistakable evidence has established the fact that a series of offensive missile sites is now in preparation on that imprisoned island. The purpose of these bases can be none other than to provide a nuclear capability against the Western Hemisphere.

Upon receiving the first preliminary hard information of this nature last Tuesday morning [October 16] at 9:00 A.M., I directed that our surveillance be stepped up. And having now confirmed and completed our evaluation of the evidence and our decision on a course of action, this Government feels obliged to report this new crisis to you in fullest detail.

The characteristics of these new missile sites indicate two distinct types of installations. Several of them include medium-range ballistic missiles, capable of carrying a nuclear warhead for a distance of more than one thousand nautical miles. Each of these missiles, in short, is capable of striking Washington, D.C., the Panama Canal, Cape Canaveral, Mexico City, or any other city in the southeastern part of the United States, in Central America, or in the Caribbean area.

Additional sites not yet completed appear to be designed for intermediate-range ballistic missiles—capable of traveling more than twice as far—and thus capable of striking most of the major cities in the Western Hemisphere, ranging as far north as Hudson's Bay, Canada, and as far south as Lima, Peru. In addition, jet bombers, capable of carrying nuclear weapons, are now being uncrated and assembled in Cuba, while the necessary air bases are being prepared.

This urgent transformation of Cuba into an important strategic base—by the presence of these large, long-range, and clearly offensive weapons of sudden mass destruction—constitutes an explicit threat to the peace and security of all the Americas, in flagrant and deliberate defiance of the Rio Pact of 1947, the traditions of this nation and hemisphere, the joint resolution of the 87th Congress, the Charter of the United Nations, and my own public warnings to the Soviets on September 4 and 13. This action also contradicts the repeated assurances of Soviet spokesmen, both publicly and privately delivered, that the arms buildup in Cuba would retain its original defensive character, and that the Soviet Union had no need or desire to station strategic missiles on the territory of any other nation.

The size of this undertaking makes clear that it has been planned for some months. Yet only last month, after I had made clear the distinction between any introduction of ground-to-ground missiles and the existence of defensive antiaircraft missiles, the Soviet government publicly stated on September 11 that, and I quote, "the armaments and military equipment sent to Cuba are designed exclusively for defensive purposes," and, I quote the Soviet government, "there is no need for the Soviet government to shift its weapons for a retaliatory blow to any other country, for instance Cuba," and that, and I quote the government, "the Soviet Union has so powerful rockets to carry these nuclear warheads that there is no need to search for sites for them beyond the boundaries of the Soviet Union." That statement was false.

Only last Thursday, as evidence of this rapid offensive buildup was already in my hand, Soviet Foreign Minister Gromyko told me in my office that he was instructed to make it clear once again, as he said his government had already done, that Soviet assistance to Cuba, and I quote, "pursued solely the purpose of contributing to the defense capabilities of Cuba," that, and I quote him, "training by Soviet specialists of Cuban nationals in handling defensive armaments was by no means offensive," and that "if it were otherwise," Mr. Gromyko went on, "the Soviet government would never become involved in rendering such assistance." That statement also was false.

Neither the United States of America nor the world community of nations can tolerate deliberate deception and offensive threats on the part of any nation, large or small. We no longer live in a world where only the actual firing of weapons represents a sufficient challenge to a nation's security to constitute maximum peril. Nuclear weapons are so destructive and ballistic missiles are so swift, that any substantially increased possibility of their use or any sudden change in their deployment may well be regarded as a definite threat to peace.

For many years, both the Soviet Union and the United States, recognizing this fact, have deployed strategic nuclear weapons with great care, never upsetting the precarious status quo which insured that these weapons would not be used in the absence of some vital challenge. Our own strategic missiles have never been transferred to the territory of any other nation, under a cloak of secrecy and deception; and our history, unlike that of the Soviets since the end of World War II, demonstrates that we have no desire to dominate or conquer any other nation or impose our system upon its people. Nevertheless, American citizens have become adjusted to living daily on the bull's-eye of Soviet missiles located inside the U.S.S.R. or in submarines.

In that sense, missiles in Cuba add to an already clear and present danger—although it should be noted the nations of Latin America have never previously been subjected to a potential nuclear threat.

But this secret, swift, and extraordinary build-up of Communist missiles—in an area well known to have a special and historical relationship to the United States and the nations of the Western Hemisphere, in violation of Soviet assurances, and in defiance of American and hemispheric policy—this sudden, clandestine decision to station strategic weapons for the first time outside of Soviet soil—is a deliberately provocative and unjustified change in the status quo which cannot be accepted by this country, if our courage and our commitments are ever to be trusted again by either friend or foe.

The 1930's taught us a clear lesson: Aggressive conduct, if allowed to grow unchecked and unchallenged, ultimately leads to war. This nation is opposed to war. We are also true to our word. Our unswerving objective, therefore, must be to prevent the use of these missiles against this or any other country, and to secure their withdrawal or elimination from the Western Hemisphere.

Our policy has been one of patience and restraint, as befits a peaceful and powerful nation, which leads a world-wide alliance. We have been determined not to be diverted from our central concerns by mere irritants and fanatics. But now further action is required—and it is under way; and these actions may only be the beginning. We will not prematurely or unnecessarily risk the costs of world-wide nuclear war in which even the fruits of victory would be ashes in our mouth—but neither will we shrink from that risk at any time it must be faced.

Acting, therefore, in the defense of our own security and of the entire Western Hemisphere, and under the authority entrusted to me by the Constitution as endorsed by the Resolution of the Congress, I have directed that the following *initial* steps be taken immediately:

First: To halt this offensive build-up, a strict quarantine on all offensive military equipment under shipment to Cuba is being initiated. All ships of any kind bound for Cuba from whatever nation or port will, if found to contain cargoes of offensive weapons, be turned back. This quarantine will be extended, if needed, to other types of cargo and carriers. We are not at this time, however, denying the necessities of life as the Soviets attempted to do in their Berlin blockade of 1948.

Second: I have directed the continued and increased close surveillance of Cuba and its military build-up. The foreign ministers of the OAS [Organization of American States] in their communiqué of October 6, rejected secrecy on such matters in this hemisphere. Should these offensive military preparations continue, thus increasing the threat to the hemisphere, further action will be justified. I have directed the armed forces to prepare for any eventualities; and I trust that in the interest of both the Cuban people and the Soviet technicians at the sites, the hazards to all concerned of continuing this threat will be recognized.

Third: It shall be the policy of this nation to regard any nuclear missile launched from Cuba against any nation in the Western Hemisphere as an attack by the Soviet Union on the

United States, requiring a full retaliatory response upon the Soviet Union.

Fourth: As a necessary military precaution, I have reinforced our base at Guantánamo, evacuated today the dependents of our personnel there, and ordered additional military units to be on a stand-by alert basis.

Fifth: We are calling tonight for an immediate meeting of the organ of consultation under the Organization of American States, to consider this threat to hemispheric security and to invoke Articles 6 and 8 of the Rio Treaty in support of all necessary action. The United Nations Charter allows for regional security arrangements—and the nations of this hemisphere decided long ago against the military presence of outside powers. Our other allies around the world have also been alerted.

Sixth: Under the Charter of the United Nations, we are asking tonight that an emergency meeting of the Security Council be convoked without delay to take action against this latest Soviet threat to world peace. Our resolution will call for the prompt dismantling and withdrawal of all offensive weapons in Cuba, under the supervision of UN observers, before the quarantine can be lifted.

Seventh and finally: I call upon Chairman Khrushchev to halt and eliminate this clandestine, reckless, and provocative threat to world peace and to stable relations between our two nations. I call upon him further to abandon this course of world domination, and to join in an historic effort to end the perilous arms race and transform the history of man. He has an opportunity now to move the world back from the abyss of destruction —by returning to his government's own words that it had no need to station missiles outside its own territory, and withdrawing these weapons from Cuba—by refraining from any action which will widen or deepen the present crisis—and then by participating in a search for peaceful and permanent solutions.

This nation is prepared to present its case against the Soviet threat to peace, and our own proposals for a peaceful world, at any time and in any forum—in the OAS, in the United Nations, or in any other meeting that could be useful—without limiting our freedom of action. We have in the past made strenuous efforts to limit the spread of nuclear weapons. We have proposed the elimination of all arms and military bases in a fair and effective disarmament treaty. We are prepared to discuss new proposals for the removal of tensions on both sides—including the possibilities of a genuinely independent Cuba, free to determine its own destiny. We have no wish to war with the Soviet Union—for we are a peaceful people who desire to live in peace with all other peoples.

But it is difficult to settle or even discuss these problems in an atmosphere of intimidation. That is why this latest Soviet threat—or any other threat which is made either independently or in response to our actions this week—must and will be met with determination. Any hostile move anywhere in the world against the safety and freedom of peoples to whom we are committed—including in particular the brave people of West Berlin —will be met by whatever action is needed.

Finally, I want to say a few words to the captive people of Cuba, to whom this speech is being directly carried by special radio facilities. I speak to you as a friend, as one who knows of your deep attachment to your fatherland, as one who shares your aspirations for liberty and justice for all. And I have watched and the American people have watched with deep sorrow how your nationalist revolution was betrayed—and how your fatherland fell under foreign domination. Now your leaders are no longer Cuban leaders inspired by Cuban ideals. They are puppets and agents of an international conspiracy which has turned Cuba against your friends and neighbors in the Americas—and turned it into the first Latin American country to become a target for nuclear war—the first Latin American country to have these weapons on its soil.

These new weapons are not in your interest. They contribute nothing to your peace and well-being. They can only undermine it. But this country has no wish to cause you to suffer or to impose any system upon you. We know that your lives and land are being used as pawns by those who deny you freedom.

Many times in the past, the Cuban people have risen to throw out tyrants who destroyed their liberty. And I have no doubt that most Cubans today look forward to the time when they will be truly free—free from foreign domination, free to choose their own leaders, free to select their own system, free to own their own land, free to speak, and write, and worship without fear or degradation. And then shall Cuba be welcomed back to the society of free nations and to the associations of this hemisphere.

My fellow citizens, let no one doubt that this is a difficult and dangerous effort on which we have set out. No one can foresee precisely what course it will take or what costs or casualties will be incurred. Many months of sacrifice and self-discipline lie ahead—months in which both our patience and our will will be tested—months in which many threats and denunciations will keep us aware of our dangers. But the greatest danger of all would be to do nothing.

The path we have chosen for the present is full of hazards, as all paths are—but it is the one most consistent with our character and courage as a nation and our commitments around the world. The cost of freedom is always high—but Americans have always paid it. And one path we shall never choose, and that is the path of surrender or submission.

Our goal is not the victory of might, but the vindication of right—not peace at the expense of freedom, but both peace *and* freedom, here in this hemisphere, and, we hope, around the world. God willing, that goal will be achieved.

SOME VIEWS ON THE NATION'S ECONOMY

JOBS AND PROSPERITY [1]

NELSON A. ROCKEFELLER [2]

With the apparent easing of international tensions in late 1962, political leaders gave increasing attention to domestic and fiscal issues. A presidential campaign is not far off. State and national officials know that a strong legislative program at the domestic level is good, not only for the country, but for political aspirants as well. So executive and congressional sights were leveled carefully on the home scene.

Of dominant concern was the nation's economic health. Critics recall that in the 1960 campaign, John F. Kennedy made much of the necessity for stepping up the country's growth rate. While there has been progress, neither the Republicans nor the Democrats are wholly satisfied with the achievements. Near the close of the second session of the 87th Congress, the President announced that he would in 1963 call for an across-the-board tax cut, the aim of which would be to quicken the economic pulse of the nation. This goal seemed to have a certain priority in 1963, just as the Trade Expansion Act, giving him broad authority to cut or remove tariffs deemed detrimental to world trade, had in 1962.

On December 5, 1962, Governor Nelson A. Rockefeller of New York, a likely front-runner for the Republican presidential nomination in 1964, launched a vigorous attack on the accomplishments and policies of the Kennedy Administration. In an address before the sixty-seventh annual Congress of American Industry, National Association of Manufacturers, in New York City, Governor Rockefeller applauded certain goals of the Administration, but questioned seriously the ways so far recommended of realizing them:

> The President predicted last January that the Federal budget would yield a surplus of $463 million, based on an estimated gross national product of $570 billion for the current year. But it now appears that the GNP will not be more than $554 billion—and that there will be a budget deficit of $7.8 billion instead of a surplus.

[1] Text furnished by Daniel F. Barr, assistant press secretary to Governor Rockefeller, with permission for this reprint.

[2] For biographical note, see Appendix.

To have achieved a GNP of $570 billion would have required private investment during 1962 between $45 and $46 billion. As it is, it will only total about $37 billion.

This failure to stimulate greater private investment is the crucial matter in relation to growth and increased employment. The rate of unemployment today is far too high.

Mr. Rockefeller cited the experience of New York State during the past four years in restoring fiscal integrity and developing a climate favorable to accelerated economic growth. He rejected the notion that "massive Government spending" will bring about economic improvement. "The basic lag is in the rate of investment for modernization and expansion of our industrial plant"; the "real need is for greater investment incentives adequate to promote a desirable rate of plant modernization and replacement."

Governor Rockefeller commended the President for urging an overhaul of the Federal tax structure. However, he pointed out,

everyone is thinking about how the promised tax cuts will benefit him or her. I guess the one thing we can be sure of is that nobody is going to be entirely satisfied. The greatest mistake we could make at this time would be a tax cut directed solely to stimulating the economy through larger deficit spending.

Whether or not, as the U.S. News & World Report indicated, Governor Rockefeller "jumped into the [political] race with what amounted to a keynote speech," is conjectural. But that he added spark to a continuing controversy over Federal spending, is certain.

Although he did not refer to him by name, there was no doubt that President Kennedy had Governor Rockefeller in mind when he gave a speech on December 14, 1962, before the Economic Club of New York. As if to answer a claim set forth by Mr. Rockefeller, the President referred specifically to New York State:

In this state the rate of insured unemployment has been persistently higher than the national average, and the increases in personal income and employment have been slower here than the nation as a whole. You have seen the tragedy of chronically depressed areas upstate, unemployed young people, and I think this might be one of our most serious national problems, unemployed young people, those in their twenties, one out of four unemployed, particularly those of the minority groups, roaming the streets of New York and our other great cities, and others on relief at an early age, with the prospect that in this decade we will have between 7 and 8 million school dropouts coming in the labor market.

The President listed three tests to which new tax legislation—the central theme of his address—should conform:

It should reduce net taxes by a sufficiently early date and a sufficiently large amount to do the job required. . . .

[It] must increase private consumption as well as investment. . . . When consumers purchase more goods, plants use more of their capacity, men are hired instead of laid off, investment increases and profits are high. Corporate tax rates must also be cut to increase incentives and the availability of investment capital. . . .

[It] should improve both the equity and the simplicity of our present tax system.

Affirming the Administration's determination to protect the nation's security and accelerate its economic growth, the President declared:

Our true choice is not between tax reduction, on the one hand, and the avoidance of large Federal deficits, on the other. It is increasingly clear that no matter what party is in power, so long as our national security needs keep rising, an economy hampered by restrictive tax rates will never produce enough revenues to balance our budget just as it will never produce enough jobs or enough profits. Surely the lesson of the last decade is that budget deficits are not caused by wild-eyed spenders but by slow economic growth and periodical recessions and any new recession would break all deficit records.

In short, it is a paradoxical truth that tax rates are too high today and tax revenues are too low and the soundest way to raise revenues in the long run is to cut rates now.

In his State of the Union Message of January 14, 1063, the President formally called for "a substantial reduction and revision in Federal income taxes" which would total about $13.5 billion "phased over three calendar years," and for reforms which would produce about $3.5 billion. He declared that such a program will "temporarily increase the deficit but can ultimately end it."

Mr. Rockefeller has continued his criticism of the Kennedy Administration's efforts to get the economy moving. Excepting his appraisals of the Government's foreign policy and its attitude toward the unresolved condition in Cuba, he has relied heavily upon the theme of fiscal responsibility, developed in the speech of December 5, 1962, to set a pattern of Republican strategy for the preconvention months immediately ahead.

In his commencement address at Yale University last June, President Kennedy urged upon the nation "a serious dialogue of the kind which has led in Europe to such fruitful collaboration among all the elements of economic society and to a decade of unrivaled economic progress."

I want to join in this dialogue today as governor of a large industrial state and as head of an administration which has spent the past four years promoting such collaboration and in achieving such economic progress on the basis of restoration of fiscal integrity and a climate favorable to the growth of private enterprise within the state. This program of action was endorsed by the people at the polls just a month ago.

Future economic progress in the state, however, is importantly related to national economic growth. Therefore, I want to talk with you today about the need for accelerated national growth, factors controlling it, and policies required to achieve it.

The economic objectives of the national Administration were clearly set forth by President Kennedy when he declared at Detroit in the fall of 1960 that "we are going to have to grow at the rate of 5 per cent a year to keep you working and your children working."

He has subsequently held that a yearly growth rate of 4.5 per cent is "well within our capability," and his Council of Economic Advisers has supported this statement.

I applaud these goals, but it is plain that the methods used to achieve them have been lacking, as we have been falling far short of achieving them as a nation.

Over the past six years, in fact, this nation's economic growth rate has been in the neighborhood of only 2.5 per cent.

The gap between goal and performance is nowhere better illustrated than in the Federal budget for fiscal 1963.

The President predicted last January that the Federal budget would yield a surplus of $463 million, based on an estimated gross national product of $570 billion for the current year. But it now appears that the GNP will not be more than $554 billion —and that there will be a budget deficit of $7.8 billion instead of a surplus.

To have achieved a GNP of $570 billion would have required private investment during 1962 between $45 and $46 billion. As it is, it will only total about $37 billion.

This failure to stimulate greater private investment is the crucial matter in relation to growth and increased employment.

The rate of unemployment today is far too high. Where it was predicted last January that national unemployment would be reduced to approximately 4 per cent by the end of the fiscal year next June, the national rate stands currently at a seasonally adjusted 5.5 per cent and shows little present promise of dropping to 4 per cent by next June.

Thus labor sees a lack of prospects for a full-employment economy. It faces automation without adequate growth to provide increasing job opportunities. It is therefore turning to the concept of a thirty-five hour week.

But shorter work hours without a comparable increase in productivity, which requires accelerated capital investment, could only place us at a further competitive disadvantage, costwise, in world markets.

This is also intimately related to our inability to achieve a balance in international payments. While our international payments deficit for 1962 may be about half a billion dollars less than in 1961, the deficit is likely to total about $2 billion—leaving us still in a disturbing position.

These are objective facts relating to our current national economic life. These are facts that must be faced squarely, because the lag in our national growth rate seriously affects our future and the future strength and vitality of the free world.

II

In seeking the answers to these problems, I believe that our experience in New York State has an important bearing on this subject.

Four years ago, when I took office as governor of New York, there were 600,000 men and women unemployed in this state, industry was in flight and the state faced a potential deficit of $700 million in the coming year (fiscal 1959-1960).

During the past four years, we have restored fiscal integrity by cutting unnecessary expenditures, instituting rigid economies, raising personal income and certain excise taxes, and putting in individual income tax withholding. The result is that we have had a balanced budget and a surplus each year, and have reduced tax-supported state debt by $85 million during the four-year period.

We have developed a climate favorable to the acceleration of economic growth through a series of seventy steps, both legislative and executive, including selective tax relief to remove impediments and increase incentives to growth of business, industry, and agriculture. Confidence has been restored.

The resulting record of the past four years reveals:

1. $8 billion of private capital invested in New York State;
2. A total of 2,278 new and expanded industrial plants;
3. A net increase of employment since January 1, 1959, of 450,000 jobs;
4. Personal incomes up $6.3 billion this year over 1958;
5. A 48 per cent increase in electric power capacity;
6. A 30 per cent increase of income from tourism—making it a $2.7 billion industry this year.

This represents a greatly accelerated rate of economic growth in New York State.

Where the state's unemployment rate had been consistently higher than the national rate during the prior administration, it has been lower than the national rate for 23 of the past 28 months.

The day I took office, the state unemployment rate was 7.7 per cent and the national rate was 7 per cent. In September of this year, the state rate was 4.5 per cent and the national rate was 4.9 per cent. (These figures are without seasonal adjustment.)

Where the rate of increase in the real personal income of the people of New York State lagged behind the national average during the prior administration, in the past four years it has been increasing more rapidly than the national rate.

The growth in production and employment within the framework of a stable tax structure has resulted in increased state revenues.

This in turn has made it possible to meet urgent social needs in the state on a pay-as-you-go basis during the past four years—to raise state aid to public schools by 60 per cent, to higher education by 260 per cent, and to triple the mileage of highway construction.

Our goal for the next four years is the encouragement of further growth in the private sector so as to produce a net increase of 500,000 more jobs in this state—and we have various new measures planned to encourage this including accelerated depreciation allowances.

But we are squarely up against the fact that further major acceleration in the rate of economic growth and the rate of increased job opportunities in New York State depends importantly on Federal policies—on what is done in terms of the nation as a whole to remove Federal impediments to economic growth and to increase Federal incentives for individual initiative, investment of private capital, and expansion of free enterprise.

This is why, as governor of New York, I have been following with such interest and concern the statements of Federal objectives affecting economic growth, and Federal actions in this area, with, naturally, particular concern for their impact on New York State.

III

The question is: Why are we failing as a nation to achieve a more rapid rate of economic growth and a more rapid expansion of job opportunities?

The weakness in the current recovery poses a real danger in the face of last January's optimistic forecasts, for it encourages those theorists who hold that the logical cure is to increase Government spending in order to shore up purchasing power and stimulate growth.

I completely reject these notions.

Economic growth cannot be achieved by such massive Government spending. This panacea has failed every time it has been tried throughout our history.

Those who argue that massive Government spending provides the only route toward accelerated economic growth espouse policies that historically have created creeping inflation, economic distortions and Government controls—demonstrably retarding rather than promoting growth in every free country in which they have been tried.

The fundamental problem we confront today is neither a lag in consumer purchasing power nor a lag in Government spending. Quite the contrary; both have increased rapidly.

The basic lag is in the rate of investment for modernization and expansion of our industrial plant.

Where we have excess capacity today, it is not due to any general overexpansion, but is due to the lag in the over-all economy, which reflects most importantly the lag in the capital goods area.

The real need is for greater investment incentives adequate to promote a desirable rate of plant modernization and replacement, which in turn would support expanded activity and increased employment in the capital goods industry, the area of the economy which is now lagging the most.

The drop in our average growth rate in the later postwar years has been directly related to the low rate of business investment in new plant and equipment necessary to increase efficiency, reduce production costs and improve our competitive position in world markets.

One of the principal causes of this lag in investments has been the fall-off in profits since 1955.

Some people seem to forget that our whole system of private enterprise is a profit and loss system—and that the hope of a profit is the incentive that makes it go.

The squeeze on profits is reducing the incentive necessary to achieve our real economic potential—for the expectation of future profits is vital to the decision to invest, profits are essential to provide funds for investment, and investment is crucial to producing economic expansion and more and better jobs.

Since the early postwar years, net profits as a per cent of the sales dollar are down from 5 per cent to 3 per cent. In fact, in terms of real income, net corporate profits have declined about 10 per cent since 1950. While many factors are related to the profits squeeze and the investment lag, Federal taxation and depreciation allowances are of major significance.

The tax structure in the United States today does not provide sufficient opportunity for accumulation of investment capital necessary to promote the growth we need.

It is significant that, in the United States, taxes on personal and corporate incomes amount to 83.4 per cent of all Federal Government levies.

This is by far the highest percentage among the central government levies of fifteen leading commercial nations of the free world.

The 83.4 per cent of total revenue derived from Federal income taxes in the United States compares with 60.2 per cent received by the central government in West Germany, 55.3 per cent in the United Kingdom, 51.7 per cent in France.

The same pattern holds true in relation to our depreciation allowances.

Our foreign competitors still get a better break from their governments, in spite of some United States progress this year.

The net result is that our competitors are investing a far larger percentage of their gross national product than we are in the construction of more modern and efficient plants.

The effect of this is a progressive weakening of our competitive position in world markets.

For example, machinery and equipment investment in 1960, expressed as a percentage of GNP, was 12.1 per cent in West Germany, 9.1 per cent in the United Kingdom, 8.4 per cent in France—and 5.5 per cent in the United States.

These percentages all represent increases for the three foreign nations over the percentages for 1950—but a decrease in the case of the United States.

In the light of this situation, it is fortunate that a remarkable consensus has developed favoring a drastic overhaul of the Federal tax structure.

The President is to be commended for advocating such an overhaul, but the important question is: What criteria do we use in determining the area, the nature and the extent of the cuts to be made, and the degree of reforms to be accomplished?

Everyone is thinking about how the promised tax cuts will benefit him or her. I guess the one thing we can be sure of is that nobody is going to be entirely satisfied.

The greatest mistake we could make at this time would be a tax cut directed solely to stimulating the economy through larger deficit spending.

In my opinion, the basic purpose of a tax cut should be to stimulate the growth of the economy through increased incentives for investment in research and development, plant modernization and expansion, resulting in increased employment and take-home pay, and improved social benefits for the community as a whole. Only thus can we achieve economic and social growth on a sound, stable and dynamic basis.

To minimize the danger of a greatly increased Federal deficit resulting from the tax cut, tremendous emphasis must be placed on elimination of waste in Government, on more businesslike management of Government affairs, and on effective restraints on Government spending without, of course, jeopardizing our national defense requirements.

I'm sure the latter can be accomplished because in the course of the first two fiscal years of this Administration, nondefense spending will be up 20 per cent—almost twice the percentage increase of national defense spending.

In terms of dollars, this means a $7 billion increase in nondefense spending as against an increase of $5.2 billion for national defense.

For example, Federal civilian payrolls are already up by 124,000 persons, costing $1.6 billion for salaries alone.

If we are to restore confidence, the goal of a balanced budget in the good years should be paid more than lip service.

The current focus on Federal tax cuts as an important element of economic growth must not blur our awareness of the other factors which so fundamentally affect the hundreds of thousands of individual decisions, made daily throughout the nation, that add up collectively to growth, to stagnation, or to retreat in our economy.

Basic among these factors is the need for an understanding and faith and belief in our economic system at all levels of government.

Let no one forget that it is the system of individual initiative and private enterprise that has kept us free, made us the world's most powerful nation, and has brought the American people to the highest standard of living of any nation in the recorded history of civilized man.

The quickest way to undermine this system is through capricious, or arbitrary, punitive administrative action at any level of government—through a government of men rather than a government of laws.

Private enterprise can only operate efficiently within a framework of laws, administrative actions and attitudes which create confidence and encourage economic growth.

Only thus can we achieve the goal of a full-employment economy with equal opportunity and full utilization of the talents of all.

Here is the basis for increased productivity of our workers, for higher real wages, for higher standards of living for our people.

Sound economic growth is the only basis on which American products can compete in world markets and on which the Government can meet its national defense responsibilities and the social needs of a growing population.

Such an economy is the basis of enduring strength for a free people at home and abroad.

You in this room today represent an important segment of the managerial genius of industrial America which has done so much to make this strength possible. The nation owes you much.

Your driving energy and imagination, your faith in the future of America, coupled with the unique skills and dedication of American labor and the creativity of our scientists and technicians, are foundation stones of human liberty in the world.

Our Founding Fathers gave their lives to achieve freedom for this nation, based on their abiding faith in the worth and dignity of each individual.

God grant us the wisdom to set national policies which will preserve and extend these values for our children and our children's children.

THE PUBLIC INTEREST IN UTILITY REGULATION [3]

RAY E. UNTEREINER [4]

The term "public interest" has been much in the news during recent years. Regulatory bodies and executive officers have either inquired or specified where private decision and public interest come to a parting of the ways. Questions have arisen over the programing practices of network television; over the projected rises in the prices of steel; over the actions of agencies controlling the publicly owned resources of land and forest; over the effect of prolonged strikes in critical and noncritical, if there be such, industries. Behind all of these and other controversies lurked the prospect, real or imagined, of governmental encroachment upon private initiative and action.

In an address before the Iowa State Conference on Public Utility Valuation and Rate Making, at Ames, Iowa, on May 2, 1963, Ray E. Untereiner spoke of the inseparability of economic and personal freedom; and by using the public utilities as examples, he underscored the necessity for "teamwork between public authority and private business."

> The basic change in our national life [he stated] is that big and virtually omnipotent government is here. And it is here to stay. It is something we shall have to adjust to in all our social arrangements. In point today, is the fact that the private enterprise system will have to be adapted to it, if it is to survive.

In this new day, Mr. Untereiner declared, "when the power of government is supreme and the serious threat to the public welfare is that we may lose the proved advantages of the economic freedom and individualism that is our heritage, a change of emphasis is called for." The "paramount public interest in regulation today is the reinvigoration . . . of the principles and institutions of the American system of private business enterprise."

A professor of economics at the California Institute of Technology, Mr. Untereiner speaks from wide experience. Consultant to the Atomic Energy Commission from 1959 to 1961, and a member of the California Public Utilities Commission from 1954 to 1958, he brings to his subject a firsthand familiarity with the thorny problems of regulation. Students

[3] Text furnished by Mr. Untereiner, with permission for this reprint.

[4] For biographical note, see Appendix.

of public address will be interested to know, moreover, that for some twelve years he directed debate teams, in addition to his other duties, at Huron College and at the California Institute of Technology.

I've wondered—as you will—why I'm here. Some of you, before I'm through, will be asking why Iowa imports corn. Probably, I'm an exhibit. The rest of you are all experts. Everything that's been said here has been clear and meaningful to you. But selling yourselves on what's right in regulation may not solve your problems. You've got to make an impact on outsiders like me—the people who elect your regulators or the executives who appoint them. Listening to me may send you away with a realization that getting better regulation won't be quite as easy as it may have seemed in the rarefied atmosphere of this conference.

I could cover my subject—The Public Interest in Regulation—in one short sentence. I could say, "There isn't much," and let it go at that. But that would be to denigrate the loftiest cliché in the established ritual of regulation. I've been on a commission. I know that the expression "in the public interest" has an esoteric connotation. These are the magic words that sanctify decisions that, without them, wouldn't make much sense. Regulatory lag might be as eternal as it seems, if commissions were deprived of this handy and irrebuttable justification for whatever decision they happen to have arrived at.

So I shall use my full allotted time. I shall use it reminding you of a few simple and basic ideas that you know and understand so well that you probably assume that everyone else is just as familiar with them. They are ideas that ought to be—but probably aren't, and won't be unless you do something about it—of public interest.

So that you may know that I am now starting on my speech, I'll give you the sentence with which most profound—or stuffy—speeches start nowadays. *We are living in a revolutionary era.*

The last such era started in a momentous year—1776. Three events of that year laid the foundations for the modern world. The first was the industrial revolution. By coupling Watt's new steam engine to machines, man, for the first time, learned to use natural power effectively in production—and his capacity to produce increased a thousandfold. The second, was our Declaration of Independence. Here in America, we established a new kind of nation; dedicated to the ideal that all men are free and equal, and that government exists to serve them, not they to serve the government. The third, was the publication of Adam Smith's *Wealth of Nations*. It provided a new philosophy of individualism and economic freedom under which industrialization, and representative government, and the institutions of private business enterprise were to work together to build the great free nations of the Western world. France by a bloody and England by a bloodless revolution followed our example. But where the liberal revolutions of 1830 and 1848 failed, industrialization was long delayed; and political, personal and business freedom never got a foothold. The cleavage between the free and the slave nations has continued and deepened to our day.

Now we are in another—a scientific revolution. Just as the industrial revolution magnified man's muscle, today's scientific revolution is magnifying his mental capacity. Maybe electronic devices can't think—yet—but they can do all the mental legwork and free man's time for creative thought. The horizons of possible achievement seem to be rushing outward with the speed of our expanding universe. It is probably safe to say that tomorrow —if not, indeed, today—there are no insuperable technological barriers to the attainment of any material objectives on which we set our hearts. If there are limits to our capacity to accomplish and improve, it is not the shortcomings of technology that impose them. A more serious barrier is imposed by our lethargy in adapting ourselves to our new environment.

Changing technology seems to demand changes in the social arrangements by which we order our lives; in government, and business, and social organization. In the earlier revolution, our Founding Fathers and the new economists laid down sound guidelines for the necessary changes. But today's social scientists —that's my field—have simply not kept up with the physical scientists. Until we learn to live with the new technology, we cannot reap its full benefits. We have already seen evidence of this; and not only in the devotion of so much of our talent to instruments of destruction. Just as the Luddite rioters, in the early days, sought to prevent mechanization by smashing the machines, there are those today who would prevent automation by insisting on job security for jobs that are becoming obsolete.

What has all this to do, you may be asking, with the subject of The Public Interest in Regulation? I think it has a great deal to do with it. In a period of change, the changes we adopt will shape our future. And regulated business is on the new frontier of change.

We, in the United States, adhered faithfully to the concept of business freedom for a century. The courts held, for example, that even railroads were private enterprises, conducted for making profits; and that the political authorities had no right to interfere with them or prescribe their rates. But in 1877, in *Munn* v. *Illinois*, the Supreme Court took a new tack. It drew a sharp line between two kinds of business enterprises. It held that, while most businesses are purely private, some few, with special characteristics, are "affected with a public interest." These—the public utilities—the Court held to be subject to direct Government regulation as to rates and service. When regulative duties became too onerous for the legislators, they delegated them to the commissions with which we are all so familiar. The authority of these commissions has become well established, very broad, and perhaps a little arbitrary. But their jurisdiction has been carefully confined to the public utilities.

For all other kinds of business, competition was to do the regulating. The Sherman Act of 1890 set the basic policy at the Federal level. The political authority was to be used to prevent combinations in restraint of trade and monopolizing; but otherwise to keep its hands off private business. For almost two generations, that policy was adhered to. Various states tried to regulate ice and gasoline distribution, and employment and theater ticket agencies, and other nonutility businesses. In every instance, the Supreme Court held such attempts to be in violation of the Constitution.

That was the law until 1934. Then, in *Nebbia* v. *New York,* in sanctioning the fixing of milk prices by public authority, the Supreme Court declared, in effect, that *any* business is "affected with a public interest" if the legislature, in enacting regulatory legislation, declares it to be so. Within a few years, in its 1937 session, the same Court began to hold that almost anything the Federal Government does in the way of regulating business is constitutional.

So here we are. The public utilities are still a special case, to which "all-out" government regulation is applied. But the constitutional guarantees of freedom for other businesses have been interpreted away. The freedom they still enjoy exists by sufferance, not as an inalienable right. They can be deprived of it at any time, and brought under the dictatorship of government, at the whim of the legislative authorities. They can no longer rely on the Supreme Court to maintain the business rights and freedom we once thought firmly imbedded in the Constitution. The future of the free economy on which this country grew to greatness is uncertain.

I don't know whether private enterprise capitalism is the best of all possible economic systems. I only know that it is the only system under which free men have ever managed to cooperate voluntarily to earn a decent living. I don't know whether the American people still want freedom; whether they have the courage to accept its risks and responsibilities, and the self-reliance to make their own decisions and create their own welfare by their own efforts. I have to assume that they do. I have nothing to say, if they do not. And I do believe they know, when they give it honest thought, that economic and personal freedom are inseverable. Kept men are never free.

So we are in a period of change. We cannot go back, and we cannot stand still. But we can shape the changes to conformity with our national goals and aspirations. The basic change already manifest in our national life is that big and virtually omnipotent government is here. And it is here to stay. It is something we shall have to adjust to in all our social arrangements. In point today, is the fact that the private enterprise system will have to be adapted to it, if it is to survive. How can this be done?

Only in the area of the public utilities and their regulation, have we had any significant experience in teamwork between public authority and private business. Only in that area has a start been made toward the working out of ground rules under which government can exercise its power as needed, without preventing the effective functioning of business. There's room for much improvement; but I think both the regulators and the regulated are trying to do a job. It could be that what they do will shape the future of all business. Even if this be not so, the regulated industries themselves are so significant a segment of our economy that what happens to the enterprise system in those industries will vitally affect the national welfare. In view of this, I cannot speak of the public interest in regulation in terms of dollars chiseled off a new rate base, or niggardliness in a rate of return, or pennies saved on a monthly bill, however deserving of attention these details may be to you who are specialists. To me as a citizen, the true and abiding public interest in regulation can be expressed only in terms of the preservation of the business freedom that undergirds the personal freedom of Americans. It is to that fundamental issue, it seems to me, that you in this room —on both sides of the regulatory fence—should be giving your best thought.

I haven't—and you may guess why—left much time for specifics. But let's just touch on the impact of regulation on the three institutions considered basic to a private enterprise economy.

The first is private property. That utility property has been "dedicated to public use" does not alter the fact that it is privately built and owned, and its owners are entitled to fair compensation for its use. This is the law, and the courts have repeatedly recognized it. But what is "fair compensation"? The courts will not intervene unless a commission-fixed rate is clearly confiscatory of a utility's property. Is the minimum nonconfiscatory rate, then, a fair one? Some commissioners have openly taken that position, and others have endorsed it by their rate decisions. But will minimum nonconfiscatory rates suffice to maintain a utility's property?

Investors seem increasingly to favor the common stock of growth companies. A growth company must have profits above its dividend requirements, to plow back into the business. It is a rare utility than can qualify. The typical pay-out ratio is 75 per cent or higher. I suspect that most utilities, if they dared retain 50 per cent of their earnings as many industrial companies do, would face a commission investigation looking to a reduction of their rates.

Utilities stocks have been attractive to investors in the past. But that may have been in part because, while they couldn't keep pace with industrials in a rising market, they provided, both incomewise and valuewise, some hedge against deflation and depression. If Big Government succeeds in its policy of preventing future recessions by perpetual inflation, utility equities may lose this appeal. The prescribed depreciation methods preclude their charging to their customers, in any extended period of inflation, the actual value of the property used up in serving them; and the possibility that new issues may be required for plant replacement presents a constant threat of dilution of outstanding equity. The time may well be near when the utilities will find themselves seriously handicapped in their access to capital markets; and in their ability, on any reasonable basis, to maintain their property. I suggest that regulation "in the public interest" dictates, and very soon, a reappraisal by regulatory commissions of the kind of return that is necessary to safeguard the institution of private property as it applies to the utilities.

What of our second basic institution—the incentive system? It may be a brutal system; for it rewards the competent and penalizes the incompetent. But it gets results; it's probably the only way to get free men to do their utmost in production; and the American people seem always to have believed in it. How diligent has regulation been in preserving it among the utilities?

Just imagine a commission decision with language like this: This utility is superbly managed. It is efficient, and progressive, and economical in its operations. Its customers get better service, at lower rates, than those of comparable utilities elsewhere. It deserves, and we allow it, a 12 per cent return.

Imagine it; because I don't think you'll find it in the reports. But why not? What is so sacrosanct about a 6 per cent—or at most a 7 per cent—return: so that that's what's allowed whether the rate base be calculated on original cost or on fair value; so that the utility furnishing the best service at the lowest rates must have its rates cut still further if it threatens to exceed it; and so that the company furnishing the poorest service at the highest rates must be given rate increases in order to achieve it? A traditional return on a rate base may be the easiest way for a commission to arrive at utility rates. If commissions are incompetent to appraise performance, it may be the safest way. But that isn't much to say for the prevailing standard. It doesn't conform to basic American principles, or our ideas of fair play.

The incentive system, if applied to utilities, should, as with unregulated industries, be a sword that cuts both ways. Rates should be set that reflect the reasonable costs, with a fair profit, of providing the particular service the utility is called on to render. Of course the reasonable costs will differ in every service area, and rates could not be uniform. But a commission willing to make the effort could arrive at fair rates for each utility. Then let the utility make the best profit it can at the rates prescribed for it. Let it make 12 per cent or 20 per cent if it's good enough; and let it go bankrupt if it's bad enough.

I wouldn't dare call for a show of hands to see if anyone here agrees. But give it a little thought. The "cost plus" type of deal the utilities now have hasn't much resemblance to the profit and loss system that keeps other industries on their toes. Utility management has demonstrated a commendable dedication to public service, to have been as efficient and progressive as it has, with so little chance of profiting from improvements. But incentives can work as well for utilities as for other business. At least, it's worth a try. I won't insist on any revolutionary innovations. But I would like, just for a starter, to see a few commissions break through the 7 per cent barrier for utilities that can earn more than that at reasonable rates, and quit trying to maintain a 6 per cent floor for utilities that can't earn it even at high rates.

Finally, the institution of individual—or business—freedom. It's limited by regulation, of course, for the utilities. But much of the paraphernalia of regulation is relatively inconsequential. Reports to be filed, and rules to be followed, and authorizations to be obtained, need not seriously affect utility operations. Even commission authority over service standards isn't very burdensome. Most utilities wouldn't render shoddy service if they could. Regulation necessarily denies freedom to the utilities in only one important respect. They cannot set their own prices for the services they sell. Probably everyone here agrees that, in the absence of effective competition, that is a proper function for the political authority.

In all other respects, the utilities are private enterprises; investor-owned, engaged in for profit, assuming risks, and facing the same kind of management decisions as nonregulated companies. They can and should be, outside the rate-fixing area, allowed about as wide a scope for management discretion as other businesses enjoy. This is not only good economics, but good law. Regulators have no legal authority to usurp the prerogatives of management.

But the regulators themselves are the first to interpret regulatory law; and the courts seem loath to overrule them. Some dictation to management finds its way into commission orders and decisions. I'll mention only one area; capital structure. Within limits, debt capital has a lower cost than equity. Commissions like low utility rates; so they are inclined to prefer debt to equity financing. It is not uncommon for them to put pressure on management; even to the point of penalizing companies with a low debt ratio by allowing them only the rates they would need if their debt ratio were as high as the commission thinks desirable. This seems to me to violate sound principles of regulation. Well-run utilities are entitled to a fair return on their investment and the risks assumed. Given that, management can increase the return—and the risk—on equity by a reasonable resort to debt. But the responsibility is that of management, and the decision should be for management to make.

I'm nearly through. I've assumed that nothing need be said to this audience about the superiorities of private over public ownership of utilities; and the necessity for constant vigilance against the trend toward collectivism directed specifically at this area of business. You who are in the utilities believe in your companies, and believe that they provide the best means by which the public need for service can be satisfied. You who are engaged in regulation know that you have the responsibility of seeing that the investor-owned utilities perform—and operate in a regulatory climate that enables them to perform—in accordance with sound standards of public service. If there be any man in regulation who has no zeal for private enterprise in the utilities field, and no dedication to its effective functioning and preservation, he betrays the high purpose for which his office was established. I'm sure that if there be any such, they do not participate in conferences such as this.

I've said nothing about the public interest in getting good utility service at low rates. No one questions this: so long as the rates are not so low as to handicap the utility in its access to capital markets, and in keeping pace with progress, and expanding with the needs of its service area, and continuing to provide dependable service not only for today's public but for tomorrow's. I've said nothing about the maxim that a commission's first duty is to the ratepayers, and that any regulator who is not "consumer-minded" is dishonest. This I believe, and so do you; although we realize that a regulator's judgment as to what is best for the ratepayers is influenced by the depth of his perception and the range of his vision of long-run objectives. These are thoughts that needed emphasis when regulation was in its infancy, and the public right to impose its will upon a segment of private industry was being established and defined. They needed emphasis when weak government was building its power to protect consumers against possible abuse by strong business.

In this new day, when the power of government is supreme and the serious threat to the public welfare is that we may lose the proved advantages of the economic freedom and individualism that is our heritage, a change of emphasis is called for. I do not belittle the work you experts do in accounting, and valuation, and financing, and other fields. The techniques of regulation should be constantly reexamined and improved. But I suggest in all sincerity that the paramount public interest in regulation today is the reinvigoration—right in the utility field where government has taken its first and longest strides, and the pattern of our future is most likely to evolve—of the principles and institutions of the American system of private business enterprise.

SCIENCE AND MAN'S FATE

MAN: THE LETHAL FACTOR [1]

LOREN EISELEY [2]

Response is generally regarded as one of the criteria for assessing the effectiveness of a speech. Did the address, either immediately or in the long run, do something to the listeners or readers which might not have occurred if they had not received the message? Did the audience indicate by action, by change of attitude or belief, that hearing or reading the words made a difference in their lives? Admittedly, it is difficult—some would say impossible—to get a reliable measure of response. The variables in the rhetorical equation are many, and the data with which the critics work are imprecise.

Without professing to scientific accuracy in the evaluation of speeches, however, we may still point up certain conclusions which appear to be supported by observation and common sense. The fact that a speech remains the subject of controversy or reflection indicates a meaningful response; it signifies a persisting concern for the ideas expressed by the speaker. If this is true, Newton N. Minow's talk "Television and the Public Interest," published in REPRESENTATIVE AMERICAN SPEECHES: 1961-1962 (pages 64-77), holds up well as an effective presentation. Two years after delivery, it still provokes discussion, furnishes quotable passages for other talks, and in general remains in memory as a germinal statement which caused persons in and out of the industry to do a bit of soul-searching. Other speeches readily come to mind. C. P. Snow's "The Moral Un-Neutrality of Science" (REPRESENTATIVE AMERICAN SPEECHES: 1960-1961, pages 41-54), continues to stir public discussion. President Kennedy's talk of October 22, 1962, on the Cuban crisis (page 7-15 of this volume) will doubtless live long as a major affirmation of national purpose. The list could easily be extended, but these examples will suggest that a speech containing an important idea, developed skillfully and clothed in attractive language, can command an audience that far outnumbers those physically present, and endure far beyond the immediate date of delivery.

[1] Published originally in *American Scientist* (51:71-83. Mr. '63) and scheduled for inclusion in the annual *Science in Progress* series, volume 14 of the collected Sigma Xi-RESA (Scientific Research Society of America) lectures. Reprinted by permission of Dr. Eiseley; Dr. Wallace R. Brode, editor of *Science in Progress;* and the Board of Editors of *American Scientist*.

[2] For biographical note, see Appendix.

"Man: The Lethal Factor," by the distinguished scholar Loren Eiseley, is one of those speeches embodying ideas which have a significant impact upon the hearer and reader. It is not the sort of address that can be examined casually while snatching furtive glances at television or musing dreamily over a word suitable for "52—down" in today's crossword puzzle. What Dr. Eiseley has to say about man's condition requires thoughtful study, and it is genuinely rewarding. University Professor of Anthropology and the History of Science in the Graduate School of Arts and Sciences of the University of Pennsylvania, Dr. Eiseley is widely known for his poetically attractive essays and books. Readers of the "Adventures of the Mind" series in the *Saturday Evening Post* will recall "An Evolutionist Looks at Modern Man," which opened that splendid collection on April 26, 1958. Among the books that have gained for him a wide reading public are *The Immense Journey, The Firmament of Time,* and the recently published *The Mind as Nature.*

The lecture here reprinted was delivered in Philadelphia on December 29, 1962, at a dinner sponsored by the Society of the Sigma Xi and Phi Beta Kappa during the annual meeting of the American Association for the Advancement of Science.

The great Olduvai Gorge in East Africa has been appropriately called the Grand Canyon of human evolution. Here a million, perhaps 2 million years of human history are recorded in the shape of successive skulls and deposits of stone tools. The elusive story of the long road man has traveled is glimpsed momentarily in eroded strata and faded bone. Olduvai is now famous all over the world. Only to those who have the habit of searching beyond the obvious, however, may it have occurred that this precipitous rift through time parallels and emphasizes a similar rift in ourselves—a rift that lies like a defacing crack across our minds and consequently many of our institutions. From its depths we can hear the rumble of the torrent from which we have ascended, and sense the disastrous ease with which both individual men and civilizations can topple backwards and be lost.

Brooding upon the mysteries of time and change, a great and thoughtful scholar, Alfred North Whitehead, many years ago recorded his thoughts in a cryptic yet profound observation. He said, in brief, "We are . . . of infinite importance, because as we perish we are immortal." Whitehead was not speaking in ordinary theological terms. He was not concerned in this passage with the survival of the human personality after death—at least as a religious conception. He was, instead, struggling with that difficult idea which he describes as the "prehension of the past," the fact that the world we know, even as it perishes, remains an elusive unfixed element in the oncoming future.

The organic world, as well as that superorganic state which exists in the realm of thought is, in truth, prehensile in a way that the inorganic world is not. The individual animal or plant in the course of its development moves always in relation to an unseen future toward which its forces are directed: the egg is broken and a snake writhes away into the grass; the acorn seedling, through many seasons, contorts itself slowly into a gnarled, gigantic oak. Similarly, life moves against the future in another sense — an evolutionary one. The creature existing now — this serpent, this bird, this man—has only to leave progeny in order to stretch out a gray, invisible hand into the evolutionary future, into the nonexistent.

With time, the bony fin is transformed into a paw, a round, insectivore eye into the nearsighted gaze of a scholar. Moreover, all along this curious animal extension into time, parts of ourselves are flaking off, breaking away into unexpected and unforeseen adventures. One insectivore fragment has taken to the air and become a vampire bat, while another fragment draws pictures in a cave and creates a new prehensile realm where the shadowy fingers of lost ideas reach forward into time to affect our world view, and with it, our future destinies and happiness.

Thus, since the dawn of life on the planet, the past has been figuratively fingering the present. There is, in reality, no clearly separable past and future either in the case of nerve and bone or within the less tangible but equally real world of history. Even the extinct dead have plucked the great web of life in such a manner that the future still vibrates to their presence. The mammalian world was, for a long time, constricted and impoverished by the dominance of the now vanished reptiles. Similarly, who knows today what beautiful creature remains potential only because of our continued existence; or what renewed manifestations of creative energy our own presence inhibits or has indeed destroyed forever.

As the history of the past unrolls itself before the eye of both paleontologist and archaeologist, however, it becomes evident, so far as the biological realm is concerned, that by far the greater proportion of once living branches on the tree of life are dead, and to this the archaeologist and historian must add dead stone, dead letters, dead ideas, and dead civilizations. As one gropes amid all this attic dust it becomes ever more apparent that some lethal factor, some arsenical poison seems to lurk behind the pleasant show of the natural order or even the most enticing cultural edifices that man has been able to erect.

In the organic world of evolution three facts, so far as we can perceive, today seem to determine the death of species: (1) the irreversibility of the organic process in time; (2) high specialization which, in the end, limits new adaptive possibilities; (3) the sudden emergence of spectacular enemies or other environmental circumstances which overwhelm or ambush a living form so suddenly that the slow adjustive process of natural selection cannot be made to function. This third principle, one could say, is the factor which, given the other two limitations upon all forms of life, will result in extinction. As a drastic example one could point to the destruction of many of the larger creatures as man has abruptly extended his sway over both hemispheres and into many different environmental zones.

The past century has seen such great accessions of knowledge in relation to these natural events, as well as a growing consciousness of man's exposure to similar dangers, that there is an increasing tendency to speculate upon our own possibilities for survival. The great life web which man has increasingly plucked with an abruptness unusual in nature shows signs of "violence in the return" to use a phrase of Francis Bacon's. The juvenile optimism about progress which characterized our first scientific years was beginning to be replaced early in this century by doubts which the widely circulated *Decline of the West* by Oswald Spengler documents only too well. As the poet J. C. Squire says, we can turn:

> the great wheel backward until Troy unburn,
> . . . and seven Troys below
> Rise out of death and dwindle. . . .

We can go down through the layers of dead cities until the gold becomes stone, until the jewels become shells, until the palace is a hovel, until the hovel becomes a heap of gnawed bones.

Are the comparisons valid? The historians differ. Is there

hope? A babble of conflicting voices confuses us. Are we safe? On this point I am sure that every person of cultivation and intelligence would answer with a resounding "No!" Spengler, and not the optimists, was right when he prophesied that this century would be one marked by the rise of dictators, great wars, and augmented racial troubles. Whether he was also right in foreseeing our century as the onsetting winter of Western civilization is a more difficult problem.

Faustian, space-loving man still hurls his missiles skyward. His tentacular space probes seem destined to palpate the farthest rim of the solar system. Yet honesty forces us to confess that this effort is primarily the product of conflict, that millions are now employed in the institutions erected to serve that conflict, that government and taxes are increasingly geared to it, that in another generation, if not now, it will have become traditional. Men who have spent their lives in the service of these institutions will be reluctant to dissolve them. A vested interest will exist on both sides of the iron curtain. The growing involution of this aspect of Western culture may well come to resemble the ingrowth and fantasies of that ritualized belief in mana which characterized late Polynesian society.

It is upon this anthropological note that I should like to examine the nature of the human species—the creature who at first glance appears to have escaped from the specialized cul-de-sac which has left his late existing primate relative, the gorilla, peering sullenly from the little patch of sheltered bush which yet remains to him. I have said that some lethal factor seems to linger in man's endeavors. It is for this reason that I venture to speak to you from a discipline which has long concerned itself with the origins, the illusions, the symbols, the folly as well as the grandeur of civilizations whose records are lost and whose temples are fallen. Yet the way is not easy. As Herman Melville has written in one great perceptive passage:

By vast pains we mine into the pyramid; by horrible gropings we come to the central room; with joy we espy the sarcophagus; but we lift the lid—and no body is there!—appallingly vacant, as vast, is the soul of man!

I have spent a sizable number of my adult years among the crude stones of man's ice age adventurings. The hard, clean flint in the mountain spring defines and immortalizes the race that preceded us better than our own erratic fabrications distinguish our time. There is as yet no sharp edge to our image. Will it be, in the end, the twisted gantries on the rocket bases, or telephone wires winding voiceless through the high Sierras, or will it be the glass from space-searching observatories pounded into moonstones in the surf on a sinking coast?

What makes the symbol, finally, for another age as the pyramids for theirs—writing for five thousand years man's hope against the sky? Before we pass, it is well to think of what our final image as a race may be—the image that will give us a kind of earthly immortality, or represent, perhaps, our final collective visage in eternity. But it is to the seeds of death within us that we must address ourselves before we dare ask this other final question of what may stand for us when all else is fallen and gone down. We shall not begin with Western society, we shall begin with man. We shall open that symbolic sepulcher of which Melville speaks. We shall grope in the roiling, tumultuous darkness, for that unplumbed vacancy which Melville termed so ironically the soul of man.

II

Since the days of Lyell and Hutton who perceived, beneath the romantic geological catastrophism of their age, that the prosaic and unnoticed works of wind and sun and water were the real shapers of the planet, science has been averse to the recognition of discontinuity in natural events.[3] Nevertheless, the rise of modern physics with its emphasis on quantum theory in the realm of particles, and even certain aspects of Mendelian genetics serve to remind us that there are still abroad in nature hidden powers which, on occasion, manifest themselves in an unpredictable fashion. Even on a more dramatic scale no one to date has been quite able satisfactorily to account for that series of rhythmic and overwhelming catastrophes which we call the ice age. It is true that we no longer cloak such mysteries in an aura of supernaturalism, but they continue to remind us, nevertheless, of the latent forces still lurking within nature.

[3] It should be said in justice to Sir Charles Lyell that in combating the paroxysmal theories which preoccupied his contemporaries he maintained, nevertheless, that "minor convulsions and changes are . . . a *vera causa*, a force and mode of operation which we know to be true."

Another of these episodes is reflected in the origins of the human mind. It represents, in a sense, a quantum step: the emergence of genuine novelty. It does so because the brain brought into being what would have been, up until the time of its appearance, an inconceivable event: the world of culture. The *mundus alter*—this intangible, faery world of dreams, fantasies, invention, has been flowing through the heads of men since the first ape-man succeeded in cutting out a portion of his environment and delineating it in a transmissible word. With that word a world arose which will die only when the last man utters the last meaningful sound.

It is a world that lurks, real enough, behind the foreheads of men; it has transformed their natural environment. It has produced history, the unique act out of the natural world about us. "The foxes have their holes," the words are recorded of the apostle Matthew, "the wild birds have their nests, but the Son of Man has nowhere to lay his head."

Two thousand years ago in the Judean desert men recognized that the instinctive world of the animals had been lost to man. Henceforward he would pass across the landscape as a wanderer who, in a sense, was outside of nature. His shadow would grow large in the night beside the glare of his red furnaces. Fickle, erratic, dangerous, he would wrest from stone and deep-veined metal, powers hitherto denied to living things. His restless mind would try all paths, all horrors, all betrayals. In the strange individual talents nourished in his metropolises, great music would lift him momentarily into some pure domain of peace. Art would ennoble him, temptation and terror pluck his sleeve. He would believe all things and believe nothing. He would kill for shadowy ideas more ferociously than other creatures kill for food, then, in a generation or less, forget what bloody dream had so oppressed him.

Man stands, in other words, between the two most disparate kingdoms upon earth: the flesh and the spirit. He is lost between an instinctive mental domain he has largely abandoned and a realm of thought through which still drift ghostly shadows of his primordial past. Like all else that lingers along the borders of one world while gazing into another we are imperfectly adapted. It is not only the sea lion from the deep waters that inches himself painfully up the shore into the unfamiliar sunlight. So does man in the deep interior of his mind occasionally clamber far up into sunlit meadows where his world is changed and where, in the case of some few—for such is the way of evolution—there is no return to lower earth. It has taken us far longer to discover the scars of evolution in our brains than to interpret the vestigial organs tucked into old crannies of our bodies, or the wounds and aches that reveal to us that we have not always walked upon two feet.

Alfred Russel Wallace, Darwin's great contemporary, perceived in 1864 that in man the rise of the most remarkable specialization in the organic world—the human brain—had, to a considerable degree, outmoded the evolution of specialized organs. The creature who could clothe himself in fur or take it off at will, who could by extension of himself into machines, fly, swim, or roll at incredible speeds, had simultaneously mastered all of earth's environments with the same physical body. Paradoxically, this profound biological specialization appeared to have produced an organ devoted to the sole purpose of escaping specialization. No longer could man be trapped in a single skin, a single climate, a single continent, or even a single culture. He had become ubiquitous. The wind wafted his little craft to the ends of the earth, seeds changed their substance under his hands, the plague hesitated and drew back before his cities. Even his body appeared destined to remain relatively stable since he had become the supremely generalized animal whose only mutability lay in his intelligence as expressed upon his instruments and weapons.

A creature who sets out upon a new road in the wilderness, however, is apt to encounter unexpected dangers—particularly if he ventures into that invisible and mysterious environmental zone, that "other world" which has been conjured up by the sheer power of thought. Man, when he moved from the animal threshold into dawning intellectual consciousness, no longer could depend upon the instinctive promptings which carry a bird upon the wing.

Although it is difficult to penetrate into that half world of the past, it is evident that order, simple order, must have rapidly become a necessity for survival in human groups across whose members the inchoate thoughts and impulses of the freed mind must have run as alarming vagaries. Man must, in fact, have walked the knife-edge of extinction for untold years. As he defined his world he also fell victim to the shadows that lay behind it. He did not accept it like the animal, as a thing given. He bowed to stone, and heard sprites in running water. The entire universe was talking about him and his destiny. He knew the powers and heard the voices. He formulated their wishes for himself. He shaped out of his own drives and timidities the rules and regulations which reintroduced into his world a kind of facsimile of his lost instinctive animal order and simplicity.

By means of custom, strengthened by supernatural enforcement, the violent and impulsive were forced into conformity. There was a way, the way of the tribe. The individual conformed or perished. There was only one way and one people, the tribe. That there were many tribes and many ways into the future no one knew, and at first in the wide emptiness of the world it scarcely mattered. It was enough that there was some kind of way or path. Even the Neanderthals had known this and had provided meat and tools that the dead might need upon their journey.

If we pause and contemplate this dim and unhistorical age for a moment, it is, as we have intimated, with the thought that it reveals a rift or schism in man's endeavors that runs through his life in many aspects and throughout his history. The great historians, like Lord Acton, have spoken of universal history as "an illumination of the soul." They have ventured to foresee the eventual unification of man and the meeting of many little histories, ultimately, in the great history of man's final unification. It may be so. Yet whether we peer backward into the cloudy mirror of the past, or look round us at the moment, it appears that behind every unifying effort in the life of man there is an opposite tendency to disruption, as if the force symbolized in the story of the Tower of Babel had been felt by man since the beginning. Eternally he builds, and across the smooth facade of his institutional structures there runs this ancient crack, this primordial flaw out of old time. We of this age have not escaped it.

Scarcely had man begun dimly and uncertainly to shape his new found world of culture than it split into many facets. Its serenity of expression, its "universal" laws were unfortunately less than those of the nature out of which he had emerged. The customs were, in reality, confined to this island, that hill fort, or the little tribe by the river bank. The people's conception of themselves was similarly circumscribed. *They* were the people. Those who made strange sounds in a different tongue or believed in other gods were queer, and at best tolerated for trading purposes if they did not encroach upon tribal territory.

In some parts of the world this remote life, untouched by self-questioning of any sort, this ancient way of small magical dealings with animals and wood spirits and man has persisted into modern times. It is a comparatively harmless but ensorcelled world in which man's innate capacities are shut up in a very tiny ring and held latent through the long passage of millennia. There are times when one wonders whether it is only a very rare accident that releases man from the ancient, hypnotic sleep into which he so promptly settled after triumphing in his first human endeavor—that of organizing a way of life, controlling the seasons and, in general, setting up his own microscopic order in the vast shadow of the natural world. It is worth a passing thought upon primitive capacities that perhaps no existing society has built so much upon so little.

Nevertheless the rift persisted and ran on. The great neolithic empires arose and extended across the old tribal boundaries. The little peoples were becoming the great people. The individual inventor and artist, released from the restrictions of a low-energy society, enriched the whole culture. The arts of government increased. As wealth arose, however, so war, in a modern sense, also arose. Conquest empires — neolithic and classic — largely erased the old tribalism, but a long train of miseries followed in their wake. Slavery, merciless exploitation such as our paleolithic ancestors never imagined in their wildest dreams, disrupted the society and in the end destroyed both the individual and the state.

There began to show across the face of these new empires not alone the symptoms of a bottomless greed, but what, in the light of times to come was more alarming: the very evident fact that, as human rule passed from the village to the empire, the number of men who could successfully wield power for long-term social purposes grew less. Moreover, the long chain of bureaucracy from the ruler to the ruled made for greater inefficiency and graft. Man was beginning to be afflicted with bigness in his affairs, and with bigness there often emerges a dogmatic rigidity. The system, if bad, may defy individual strength to change it and simply run its inefficient way until it collapses. It is here that what we may call involution in the human drama becomes most apparent.

There tend to arise in human civilization institutions which monopolize, in one direction or another, the wealth and attention of the society, frequently to its eventual detriment and increasing rigidity. These are, in a sense, cultural overgrowths, excessively ornate societal excrescences as exaggerated as some of the armor plate which adorned the gigantic bodies of the last dinosaurs. Such complications may be as relatively harmless as a hyper-developed caste system in which no social fluidity exists, or, on the contrary, as dangerous as military institutions which employ increasingly a disproportionate amount of the capital and attention of the state and its citizens.

III

In one of those profound morality plays which C. S. Lewis is capable of tossing off lightly in the guise of science fiction, one of his characters remarks that in the modern era the good appears to be getting better and the evil more terrifying. It is as though two antipathetic elements in the universe were slowly widening the gap between them. Man, in some manner stands at the heart of this growing rift. Perhaps he contains it within himself. Perhaps, as we have remarked, he feels the crack slowly widening in his mind and his institutions. He sees the finest intellects which, in the previous century, concerned themselves with electric light and telephonic communication devote themselves as whole-heartedly to missiles and supersonic bombers. He finds that the civilization which once assumed that only barbarians would think of attacking helpless civilian populations from the air has, by degree, come to accept the inevitability of such barbarism.

Hope, if it is expressed by the potential candidates for mass extermination in this age of advanced destruction, is expressed, not in terms of living, but in those of survival, such hope being largely premised on the confidence in one's own specialists to provide a nuclear blanket capable of exceeding that of the enemy. All else gives way before the technician and the computer specialist running his estimates as to how many million deaths it takes, and in how many minutes, before the surviving fragment of a nation—if any—sues for peace. Nor, in the scores of books analyzing these facts, is it easy to find a word spared to indicate concern for the falling sparrow, the ruined forest, the contaminated spring—all, in short, that spells a life in nature still to man.

As one of these technicians wrote in another connection involving the mere use of insecticides, and which I here shorten and paraphrase: "Balance of nature? An outmoded biological concept. There is no room for sentiment in modern science. We shall learn to get along without birds if necessary. After all, the dinosaurs disappeared. Man merely makes the process go faster. Everything changes with time." And so it does. But let us be as realistic as the gentleman would wish. It may be we who go. I am just primitive enough to hope that somehow, somewhere, a cardinal may still be whistling on a green bush when the last man goes blind before his man-made sun. If it should turn out that we have mishandled our own lives as several civilizations before us have done, it seems a pity that we should involve the violet and the tree frog in our departure.

To perpetrate this final act of malice seems somehow disproportionate, beyond endurance. It is like tampering with the secret purposes of the universe itself and involving not just man but life in the final holocaust—an act of petulant, deliberate blasphemy.

It is for this reason that Lewis' remark about the widening gap between good and evil takes on such horrifying significance in our time. The evil man may do has just this added significance about it—it is not merely the evil of one tribe seeking to exterminate another. It is, instead, the thought-out willingness to make the air unbreathable to neighboring innocent nations, and to poison, in one's death throes, the very springs of life itself. No greater hypertrophy of the institution of war has ever been observed in the West. To make the situation more ironic, the sole desire of every fifth-rate nascent nationalism is to emulate Russia and America—to rattle rockets, and if these are too expensive, then at least to possess planes and a parade of tanks. For the first time in history a diverse nationalism, spread like a contagion from the West, has increased in virulence and blown around the world.

A multitude of states are now swept along in a passionate hunger for arms as the only important symbol of prestige. Yearly their number increases. For the first time in human history the involutional disease of a single, modern civilization, that of the West, shows signs of becoming the disease of all contemporary societies. Such, it would appear, is one of the less beneficial aspects of the communications network which we have flung around the world. The universal understanding which has been the ultimate goal sought by the communications people, that shining Telstar through which we were to promote the transmission of wisdom, bids fair, instead, to promote unsatisfied hunger and the enthusiastic reception of irrationalities that embed themselves all too readily in the minds of the illiterate.

Man may have ceased to teeter uncertainly upon his hind legs, his strange physical history may be almost over. But within his mind he is still hedged about by the shadows of his own fear and uncertainty; he still lingers at the borders of his dark and tree-filled world. He fears the sunlight, he fears truth, he fears himself. In the words of Thomas Beddoes who looked long into that world of shadows:

> Nature's polluted,
> There's man in every secret corner of her
> Doing damned wicked deeds. Thou art, old world
> A hoary, atheistic, murdering star.

This is the dark murmur that rises from the abyss beneath us, and that draws us with uncanny fascination.

If one were to attempt to spell out in a sentence the single lethal factor at the root of declining or lost civilizations up to the present, I would be forced to say adaptability. I would have to remark, paradoxically, that the magnificent specialization of gray matter which has opened to us all the climates of the earth, which has given us music, surrounded us with luxury, entranced us with great poetry, has this one flaw: it is too adaptable. In breaking free of instinct and venturing naked into a universe which demanded constant trial and experiment, a world whose possibilities were unexplored and unlimited, man's hunger for experience became unlimited also. He has the capacity to veer with every wind, or, stubbornly, to insert himself into some fantastically elaborated and irrational social institution only to perish with it.

It may well be that some will not call this last piece of behavior adaptation. Yet it is to be noted that only extreme, if unwise, adaptability would have allowed man to contrive and inhabit such strange structures. When men in the mass have once attached themselves to a cultural excrescence which grows until it threatens the life of the society, it is almost impossible to modify their behavior without violence. Yet along with this, as I have remarked, fervid waves of religious or military enthusiasm may sweep through a society and then vanish with scarcely a trace.

It would take volumes to chronicle the many facets of this problem. It is almost as though man had at heart no image, but only images, that his soul was truly as vacant as Melville intimated in the passage I have earlier quoted. Man is mercurial and shifting. He can look down briefly into the abyss and say, smiling, "We are beasts from the dark wood. We will never be anything else. We are not to be trusted. Never on this earth. We have come from down there." This view is popular in our time. We speak of the fossil ape encrusted in our hearts.

This is one image of many that man entertains of himself. There is another left by a man who died a long time ago. I have spoken earlier of the collective symbol a civilization sometimes leaves to posterity and the difficulty one has with our own because of the rapidity with which our technology has altered, and the restless flickering of our movement from one domain of life to another.

A few months ago I read casually in my evening newspaper that our galaxy is dying. That great wheel of fire of which our planetary system is an infinitesimal part was, so the report ran, proceeding to its end. The detailed evidence was impressive. Probably, though I have not attempted to verify the figures, the spiral arm on which we drift is so vast that it has not made one full circle of the wheel since the first man-ape picked up and used a stone.

Now I saw no use in whispering behind my hand at the club, next morning, "They say the galaxy is dying." I knew well enough that man, being more perishable than stars, would be gone billions of years before the edge of the Milky Way grew dark. It was not that aspect of the human episode that moved me. Instead it was the sudden realization of what man could do on so gigantic a scale even if, as yet, his personal fate eluded him. Out there millions of light years away from earth, man's hands were already fumbling in the coal-scuttle darkness of a future universe. The astronomer was foreshortening time—just as on a shorter scale eclipses can be foretold, or an apparently empty point in space can be shown as destined to receive an invisibly moving body. So man, the short-lived midge, is reaching into and observing events he will never witness in the flesh. In a psychological second, on this elusive point we call the present, we can watch the galaxy drift into darkness.

The materiality of the universe, Whitehead somewhere remarks, is measured "in proportion to the restriction of memory and anticipation." With consciousness, memory, extended through the written word and the contributions of science, penetrates farther and farther into both aspects of time's unknown domain, that is, the past and the future. Though individual men do not live longer, we might say that the reach of mind in the universe and its potential control of the natural order is enormously magnified.

Material substance no longer dominates the spiritual life. There is not time here to explore all aspects of this fascinating subject, nor the paradoxes with which our burgeoning technology have presented us. This strange capacity of the mind upon which we exercise so little thought, however, means that man both remains within the historical order and, at the same time, passes beyond it.

We are present in history, we may see history as meaningless or purposeful, but as the heightened consciousness of time invades our thinking, our ability to free our intellects from a narrow and self centered immediacy should be intensified. It is this toward which Whitehead was directing his thought: that all responsible decisions are acts of compassion and disinterest; they exist within time and history but they are also outside of it—unique and individual and, because individual, spiritually free. In the words of Erich Frank, "History and the world do not change, but man's attitude to the world changes."

I wonder if we understand this point, for it is the crux of all my efforts in this lecture, and though I have mentioned modern thinkers, it leads straight back to the New Testament. A number of years ago in a troubled period of my life I chanced to take a cab from an airport outside a large eastern city. The way to the address I gave lay through the back streets of a run-down area of dilapidated buildings. I remember we passed a pathetic little cemetery whose smudged crosses, dating from another era, were now being encroached upon and overshadowed by the huge gray tanks of an oil refinery. The shadow of giant machines now fell daily across the hill of the dead. It was almost a visible struggle of the symbols to which I have earlier referred—the cross that marks two thousand years of Western culture, shrinking, yet still holding its little acre in the midst of hulking beams and shadows where now no sunlight ever fell.

I felt an unreasoned distaste as we jounced deeper into these narrow alleyways, or roared beneath giant bridges toward a distant throughway. Finally, as we cut hastily through a slightly more open section, I caught a glimpse of a neighborhood church —a church of evident poverty, of a sect unknown, and destined surely to vanish from that unsavory spot. It was an anachronism as doomed as the cemetery. We passed, and a moment later, as though the sign had been hanging all that time in the cab before me, instead of standing neatly in the yard outside the church, my conscious mind unwillingly registered the words:

> Christ died to save mankind.
> Is it nothing to you, all ye that pass by?

I looked at that invisible hanging sign with surprise, if not annoyance. By some I have been castigated because I am an evolutionist. In one church where I had attended as the guest of a member not long before, I had been made the covert object of a sermon in which I had recognizably played the role of a sinning scientist. I cannot deny that the role may have fitted me, but I could not feel that the hospitality, under the circumstances, was Christian. I had seen fanatical sectarian signs of ignorant and contentious sects painted on rocks all over America, particularly in desert places. I had gazed unmoved on them all.

But here on a plain white board that would not remove itself from my eyes, an unknown man in the shadow of one of the ugliest neighborhoods in America had in some manner lifted that falling symbol from the shadow of the refinery tanks and thrust it relentlessly before my eyes. There was no evading it. "Is it nothing to you?" I was being asked—I who passed by, who had indeed already passed, and would again ignore, much more sophisticated approaches to religion.

But the symbol, one symbol of many in the wilderness of modern America, still exerted its power over me—a dozen lines of thinking, past and present drew in upon me. Nothing eventful happened in the outside world. Whatever took place happened within myself. The cab sped on down the throughway.

But before my mind's eye, like an ineradicable mote, persisted the vision of that lost receding figure on the dreadful hill of Calvary who whispered with his last breath, "It is finished." It was not for Himself He cried—it was for man against eternity— for us of every human generation who perform against the future, the acts which justify creation or annul it. This is the power in the mind of man—a mind print, if you will—an insubstantial symbol which holds like a strained cable the present from falling into the black abyss of nothingness. This is why, if we possess great fortitude each one of us can say against the future he has not seen, "It is finished."

At that moment we will have passed the reach of time into a still and hidden place where it was said, "He who loses his life will find it." And in that place we will have found an ancient and an undistorted way.

SCIENCE AND MAN [4]

THEODORE M. HESBURGH [5]

In his illuminating essay "A Moral for an Age of Plenty," Jacob Bronowski, British-trained scientist and mathematician, called the conscience of the scientist "the most active morality in the world today." He declared, moreover, that "the moral problem of our century is to make the values of science as much a part of our lives as are the values which religion and literature have long glorified." But advances in science continue to pose the frightening dilemma of our time: how to use the fantastic power recently placed in man's hand, and yet control its potential fury in an armed world where peace is delicately balanced.

Oftentimes the scientist is blamed for releasing the force which now threatens to undo us. But such an assignment of responsibility is too pat. All society shares in the challenge. The scientists are acutely aware of the impact of their discoveries on society. Their special knowledge provides them with insights denied to many of us. Without assuming the role of politicians, they can and do inform their fellow men of the possible effects of scientific developments on life and environment.

But a fundamental question remains: Does science realize "its greatest human potentiality in our times?" Some doubt it. Speaking in Los Angeles on November 16, 1962, at a dinner sponsored by the California Institute of Technology in honor of the National Science Board, the Reverend Dr. Theodore M. Hesburgh called upon scientists and engineers to liberate mankind from hunger, illiteracy, and disease. President of the University of Notre Dame and one of the nation's most distinguished religious educators, Father Hesburgh granted that there are many things science and technology cannot do. But "there is one task that is made to order for them in our day, and it is to buttress freedom, to better the conditions of mankind on earth, to liberate man from his ancient servitudes, to provide for man a human situation in which he can truly manifest his dignity, practice his freedom, and follow his high spiritual calling." He urged scientists and engineers to engage in a "review of values." "Science and engineering, in our times," he continued, "are anything but mediocre."

Why then should the scientist and engineer allow them to be used for mediocre ends and to hide himself in the mass. Ours

[4] Text furnished by Father Hesburgh, with permission for this reprint.

[5] For biographical note, see Appendix.

is a time of great change, of revolutionary winds, of new break-throughs on every front. Should the one great problem, the condition of man, be deprived of breakthrough in our times? Should we pioneer in space and be timid on earth? Must we break the bonds of earth and leave man in bondage below? This, I submit, is the core problem of science and man in our times.

Students interested in further reading on the integration of science and society in recent years may wish to examine Glenn T. Seaborg's "A Scientific Society—The Beginnings," published in REPRESENTATIVE AMERICAN SPEECHES: 1961-1962 (pages 110-23); or his "Freedom and the Scientific Society: The Third Revolution," delivered at the Prelude to Independence celebration at Colonial Williamsburg, Virginia, on May 26, 1962.

I wish to address you this evening on the subject of science and man. It is a fair assumption that the majority of this audience knows much more about science and technology than I do. This being so, one might wonder why I do not drop the first part of my title of science and man. This is why: I shall not pretend to make any startling revelations in the field of science and technology; but I do want to consider this twin reality in conjunction with man and his actual world. What I have to say may not be popular, but then I never have found this to be a good reason for not saying something that should be said. Anyway, most statements that are popular and safe are also generally dull. This you should be spared.

Too often when the scientist or engineer speaks of science and technology, he speaks of them in isolation, because this is the world he knows best, in some cases, the only world he knows. Do not blame the scientist or engineer too much for this. He has grown up in a world of vastly expanding knowledge and it takes his every waking hour just to stay on top of all that is happening. If you want to dramatize the fact, remember that over 90 per cent of all the scientists who have ever lived are living today. And most of them are working at their art. *Chemical Abstracts,* for example, covered 42,000 papers in 1948, and 145,000 last year. The Armed Services Technical Information Agency furnished 113,300 reports to engineers ten years ago, as compared to over 700,000 this past year.

I do not have to assume this burden of research and reading. Perhaps I can make a virtue of this deficiency, since it leaves me time to look at the broad lineaments of science and technology by reading the headlines of movement, project and discovery, and to relate this vast human effort to deeper realities in the total world of man which is in a sense my chosen world.

I trust you will forgive me if for a few moments at this point I am autobiographical. This is a dangerous business. As St. Francis once said, speaking of oneself is like walking the tightrope. It takes balance, but it may contribute ultimately to what I have to say, so I will take the chance. Eight years ago, I had a call from the White House asking if I would accept a position on the National Science Board. I replied that I must be the wrong man since all of my education had centered on philosophy and theology. Then I was told that President Eisenhower wanted a philosophical and theological point of view represented on the Science Board. What can one say to that? I joined, and my scientific education began.

Other assignments followed subsequently to fill out the picture: the board of the Midwestern Universities Research Association, working on a new scheme in high energy physics, the Nutrition Foundation Board, the Policy Advisory Board of Argonne National Laboratory, the International Atomic Energy Agency— Atoms for Peace—and the board of the original Physical Science Study Committee, to mention a few. Our own science program at the University also filled some gaps in my scientific education. As the years passed, I suddenly found that I had many more friends among the scientists and engineers than among the philosophers and theologians. I still read the journals of my own profession, and have enjoyed those rare moments when I could be a philosopher and theologian, but the pressure has been relentless to learn more and more about science and technology. I shall never be a scientist or engineer since I started all this too late, but I have learned something of the language and the vision and the adventure of science and technology. I have also learned to respect these exacting arts and their practitioners. It is wonderful to stand on a street corner in San Francisco and have Glenn Seaborg explain the relationship between his discovery of the transuranium element of californium and the Crab Nebula as described in Chinese scientific observations of the eleventh century when this supernova occurred. These have been good years, filled with good people—especially the distinguished members of the National Science Board, including Cal Tech's outstanding president, Dr. Lee DuBridge.

Each of us must, however, be ourselves and I know you will forgive me if I see science and technology in our day through my own special spectrum of philosophy and theology. This may at first blush seem to be a negative reaction, but may I insist that it is more in the nature of a maser, magnifying natural perception manyfold, giving a wider perspective and a deeper meaning to science and technology in our day. Whatever else these past years have meant, they have made of me no enemy of science and technology, but rather a friend that would like to see these twin currents make their full and complete contribution to the life of man in our times. This will not automatically happen. In fact, if science and technology are turned in upon themselves, with no reference to the higher and deeper realities of human life and aspiration, they may ultimately become the scourge instead of the great benefactor of mankind.

It is all a matter of perspective, a simple statement, but a reality not easily perceived or appreciated. No one can deny that science and technology are the greatest and most impelling forces in twentieth century culture. Just look at what they have accomplished for this nation which has totally espoused them. We are better fed, better housed, better clothed, better medicated, longer lived than any people in the history of mankind. We have better communications, better transportation, and more electrical energy than any nation on earth. We are indeed the affluent society, almost overwhelmed by every convenience and gadget, envied and emulated by every other society that may condemn us at one moment and imitate us the next.

Our Lord once made a telling point that is amply verified today. He said: "Where your treasure is, there also will your heart be." Anyone looking at where our money is spent can easily diagnose our heart's desire. For example, this year we are spending more for research and development than was spent in the totality of our national history from the American Revolution until the end of World War II. In the past sixteen years since the war, out total expenditures for research and development have multiplied eight times, from $2.1 billion in 1946-1947, to almost $16 billion this year.

The growth of these expenditures has been even more dramatic as regards our colleges and universities. In 1940, the Federal Government was supporting research and development in our educational institutions at the annual rate of $15 million. This has now multiplied sixty times to a rate of $900 million in 1961. And this is not the total picture of support, although it is the largest segment, since the tax dollar presently supports 75 per cent of all academic research in the physical and life sciences.

There has been much study and pronouncement lately on the effect of this growing Federal support on the life and programs of the university. There is still much to be said, and it is relevant to my theme, but I shall avoid this interesting side road and keep to my main line this evening, which is not the university, but man.

Question: Is this monumental and rapidly accelerating movement towards science and technology a bad reality of our times, dangerous and prejudicial to man's better interests? Are science and technology getting out of hand? One cannot give a simple yes or no answer to these questions, for science and technology are of themselves morally neutral, neither good nor bad. Science and technology are simply means not ends, and they are only good or bad depending upon how they are used by man. This leads us to the really significant question: How well are science and technology being used by man and for man in our times?

To answer this question in any depth, one must move out of the scientific and technological dimension. The nature and destiny of man is not a scientific or technological question. It is essentially philosophical and theological. As far as man is concerned, one might say it is *the* philosophical and theological question, the basis for moral judgment about every human activity, including science and technology.

There are two classic answers to this question that stand in stark contention today. These answers are generally classified as those of East or West, as material or spiritual, as communistic or democratic, but the real answer is not quite as simple as the good guys and the bad guys, if one is truly honest. All of us like to be on the side of the angels—especially in Los Angeles, the City of the Angels. However, let us remember that this means to be on the side of honesty, and here alone do we get a glimmer of the real answer.

The communistic viewpoint on the nature and destiny of man is forthright and clear-cut. We must give them that. They view man as a simple material reality, of the earth earthy if you will, with no destiny beyond time, the pawn of deterministic causality, bereft of innate spiritual dignity and, therefore, a creature of the state with no inherent or inalienable rights. In their view, there is no question of a Creator or Divine Providence, no eternal destiny, nothing beyond matter and, therefore, the task of science and technology for them is quite simple: to create an earthly paradise by whatever procedures the state determines, without personal freedom or choice on the part of the scientist or engineer.

This is not my dream, but theirs: I merely quote their stated intentions. I am ready to concede that within this scheme, science and technology can hasten the achievement of their stated goals. Again, do not condemn science and technology for this, since as I have said, science and technology are morally neutral, ready and available to serve any goal men choose, good or evil. Men make the choice. I happen to believe that the Communist choice is evil and in so believing I think that they prostitute science and technology to goals unworthy of man as he truly is, unworthy of man's highest and truest aspirations, destructive of human dignity and freedom.

Believing this, I would sincerely like to say that we do better, that our science and technology are more attuned to a higher vision of man. But again, the picture is not quite so black or white. Our performance is not quite so clear-cut in opposition to theirs. May I go further and say that our vision of man's nature and destiny, although higher and better in statement, is often fogged by our actual performance. We may assert a more spiritual philosophy of man's nature and destiny, but in the use of science and technology, we are in practice rather selfishly committed to our own material satisfactions and survival, largely unmindful of the total human situation today.

I think it fair to say that, on balance, we Americans as persons identify ourselves with that which is best in our tradition. The American Revolution launched by the shot heard round the world; the proposition that all men are endowed by their Creator with certain inalienable rights, life, liberty and the pursuit of happiness; the vision of a free society of free men who see in freedom the opportunity to ennoble mankind everywhere. These are lofty statements. They presuppose that man is spirit as well as matter, that we have an eternal as well as temporal destiny, that we are captains of our destinies, not creatures of the state. One might further suppose, in keeping with these noble and traditional American propositions, that we would use every means at our disposal to further our high purposes for mankind: education, public policy, science and technology, too. Yet have we been as single-minded in achieving our vision as the Communists have been in realizing theirs? Are we really so much different, especially in the use of this most potent means at our disposal today, the knowledge and power of science and technology?

Much of their science and technology is used for pure military purposes, human talent and brain power dedicated to the means of destroying man. Is our record much better? We can plead defense and it is a plausible plea, but does it say everything that might be said? I am tempted here to suggest what the world-wide fraternity of scientists and engineers might do to ameliorate this tragic situation, but this would lead us too far afield at the moment. To return to our trend of thought, what of the overage, if we bypass the predominant element of military research and development? How much of what is left to expend of the resources of science and technology do we dedicate to liberating man from his ancient bondages of hunger, illness, grinding poverty, and homelessness? Page through any newspaper or magazine, listen to our radio and look at our television programs. What image do these give of the production of the white-coated army of scientists and engineers? To a hungry world we give the image of stored surpluses, better dog food, more esoteric dishes, how to eat more and still lose weight, how to have more appetite and then alleviate the effects of overeating, how to stimulate and then sedate. Better soap, better deodorants, better beer, better cigarettes, better heating and cooling, better barbiturates, better cars, better chewing gum: these seem to be the ultimate blessings that science and technology have afforded us, the highly visible trappings of our American society, the most widely advertised contributions of science and technology to modern-day America and to the world.

I fully realize that science and technology are committed in our day to tasks other than war and luxuries. There are exciting adventures in space, but even here the pressured pace and the resulting escalated costs would not be so extreme if we were not operating under the exigencies of cold war competition and military possibilities. And remember that even we and the Russians do not have infinite resources of men and money. Enormous sums of money spent on Project A cancel out the possibility of undertaking Project B, C, and D, and in this present case, almost all the way to Z. But even so, we are still doing other things, too, even if on a reduced scale: radio astronomy, oceanography, genetics, cryogenics, cybernetics, atmospheric research, high energy physics, Mohole, and others. Even so, I submit to you that what really has impact on the earth's people, outside of America, is that thanks to science and technology, we are wealthy while they are poor, we are healthy while they are diseased, we live in palaces compared to their shacks, we are well fed while they are hungry, we are educated while they are ignorant, in sum, we have the good life while they have only frustrated hopes. We may think to win them by the dazzling performance of putting men in space, but this is meager inspiration to people living in the swamps of poverty, ignorance, and disease, below the arching orbits.

As Sir Oliver Franks has stated, the real question today is not East and West, but North and South, the rich nations and the poor nations, the haves and the have-nots. Barbara Ward has amply indicated that the gap is not closing but widening, and the frustration mounts by the minute.

None of us have written the script for the condition of mankind today. But we can, if we really believe in freedom and human dignity, help create in our day a new condition of mankind, a situation in which human freedom and dignity are at least possible, and not a bitter travesty. Never before in the history of mankind has this been possible. The vast majority of mankind has ever been hungry, diseased, ignorant, poor, and badly housed. The great glory of science and technology in our day is that it now provides the means of relieving this ancient human bondage, these cruel forms of universal human slavery. Science is most nobly described in our day as the great liberator of man in his present earthly condition.

But will science and technology in our day be dedicated to this great and noble work of human liberation? The best way to approach an answer to this question is not to ask it of science and technology, which are impersonal, but to ask the men who are the scientists and the engineers, the men who create and operate the present world of science and technology. Maybe it is time for scientists and engineers to become philosophers and theologians, too, that they might question the moral impact of their work on the world of man in which they live. Is this asking too much of scientists and engineers? Ask anything less, and you reduce scientists and engineers to the level of automatons, and condemn them to the same state that we bemoan in our adversary. It really makes little practical difference if scientists and engineers in the Soviet realm are forced to dedicate their lives to utterly materialistic ends, and ours are seduced to do likewise, by financial support, by prestigious appointments, or by the wave of our present affluent culture and material preoccupations. In either case, science is prostituted to something far below its greatest human potentiality in our times. In either case, mankind is the loser, and indeed the heaviest moral condemnation may fall upon the scientists and engineers who act freely, who might have chosen differently.

I realize that both science and engineering may be a spiritually satisfying experience for the scientist and engineer, but this is not the thrust of my remarks which concern the moral and social effects of science and technology in our day. I would even say that this personal satisfaction would be greatly enhanced if the individual scientist and engineer knew that his unique efforts were part of a great human endeavor to reverse the historic inhumanity of man to man, and to make nature work for instead of against mankind. If on the other hand, the efforts of the scientist and engineer are directed towards trivial or worse ends, his personal satisfaction will have a rather pathetic hue to anyone who thinks seriously of the total human situation today.

We all admit the impact of the scientific and technological revolution in our times; but we have yet to witness the revolution of scientists and engineers. Do not be afraid of the word *revolution*. Our country began with one. And all of the new countries, a third of mankind, are now experiencing another: the revolution of rising expectations. The realization of these expectations will not come to pass without the total application of science and technology to their many problems of development.

If their expectations are frustrated, we can write off our hopes for their entrance into the world of free men. Man's spiritual potentialities are not well realized in an atmosphere of material stagnation, abysmal poverty, and general hopelessness. As St. Theresa of Avila, the great Spanish mystic, said with her characteristic good sense: "If a hungry man asks you to teach him how to pray, you had better feed him first."

Think for a moment of what would happen if the revolution of scientists and engineers should occur in our times. Suppose that our scientists and engineers really decided to make an assault on hunger: by developing both good and arid lands abroad and organizing large-scale agriculture around the world as we have in this country where 5 per cent to 10 per cent of the population feed all the rest of the people and develop huge surpluses. We have proved that it can be done, but we have been satisfied to do it mainly for ourselves. If scientists and engineers put their talents to work, do you believe that there would be 900 million illiterates in this world, with all the riches of human culture closed to them? With modern communications, one master teacher can teach millions—but it isn't being done, except in a few isolated places where it has begun without our help. What if more scientists and engineers decided to make a concerted assault on disease, through better sanitation, vaccination, nutrition and all the rest? Again, we do it for ourselves and seem largely unconcerned about the rest of humanity. We know that industrial development depends largely upon electrical energy. Africa, for example, has 40 per cent of the hydroelectrical potential of the world. But only one half of 1 per cent of the potential is developed. We balked at the Aswan Dam and let the Russians do it. Italian engineers built the Kariba, and we argued for months about the Volta in Ghana. People might legitimately ask, "Are they really interested?" The scientists and engineers in turn might blame the politicians who make the decisions, but I insist: we are committed to freedom and we are still free to work where and as we wish. Am I then suggesting that scientists and engineers take over the governance of our country? Not quite, but I am more than suggesting that scientists and engineers cannot be oblivious to the moral quality and effects of their handiwork. No one of us, as a person, likes to be used for purposes other than those of our personal choosing. This is the meaning of freedom and responsibility which is an individual, not a mass affair. Dr. Oppenheimer was, I take it, rather deeply moved when he remarked, after Hiroshima and Nagasaki, "The scientist has now known sin." Virtue and sin are the fruit of freedom, impossible without it. And freedom is a precious heritage. When we say that freedom is ours to have and to hold, we do not exclude scientists and engineers. Freedom is also indivisible. When one man or one nation is not free, all freedom in this world is endangered.

How free are the ignorant of this world, how free are the diseased, the undernourished, the homeless, the poor, those without hope for themselves and their children? There are many things that science and engineering cannot do, but there is one task that is made to order for them in our day, and it is to buttress freedom, to better the conditions of mankind on earth, to liberate man from his ancient servitudes, to provide for man a human situation in which he can truly manifest his dignity, practice his freedom, and follow his high spiritual calling. This is why I said earlier that in our day science can be the great liberator of mankind.

This will not happen, I submit, until scientists and engineers decide that this is a task of the highest priority, and that they will commit themselves to do it. Someone may remark at this point: "But we are spending billions for foreign aid." Yes, about 4 billion annually to be exact. But again, about half of this is military aid, and the 2 billion that are left seem hardly sacrificial when you compare it to the 6 billion we spend annually for tobacco, the 12 billion for alcohol, the 20 billion for that ancient pastime called gambling. I shall spare you the bill for entertainment.

I am speaking of values, and proportion, or perspective if you prefer the word. We cannot blink at the fact that there are only eighty engineers backing up our multibillion Agency for International Development, as against eight or nine thousand in our Space Agency. We cannot overlook the fact that the total seventy-eight nation budget for the International Atomic Energy Agency—the Atoms for Peace Program—is less than the cost of our single October moon shot. We spend more to produce one nuclear submarine than our total annual budget for agricultural research, and this in a world of hunger. I could multiply examples, but by now the point should be fairly obvious: the Russians may be the bad guys, but we are not automatically the good guys. We have the talent and potential for greatness, we have the great tradition of the West, a deep concern for the dignity of man, for freedom, but in the terminology of the space age, the destruct button is getting more attention from science and technology than the construct button. People are coming out second best to things.

What do we do about it—if you are still with me? Facile solutions are useless. Revolution may seem too strong a word. Yet all it means is a turnabout, in this case a review of values, not as professed but as practiced. No one can do this for the scientist or the engineer. He must do it for himself. This is the age-old burden of freedom and individual responsibility. Pasternak, in his Nobel Prize-winning novel, *Dr. Zhivago,* says that gregariousness, the mass mentality, is the refuge of the mediocre. Science and engineering, in our times, are anything but mediocre. Why then should the scientist and engineer allow them to be used for mediocre ends and to hide himself in the mass. Ours is a time of great change, of revolutionary winds, of new breakthroughs on every front. Should the one great problem, the condition of man, be deprived of breakthrough in our times? Should we pioneer in space and be timid on earth? Must we break the bonds of earth and leave man in bondage below? This, I submit, is the core problem of science and man in our times. I claim no special wisdom, no prophetic charisma, but I do sense the call of compassion to science and technology today from mankind everywhere. The question still remains, will there be this new day for mankind in our times?

Until this day dawns, whatever the blessed condition of our beloved America, our political philosophy will be sterile abroad, our theological vision will atrophy, and our magnificent vision of man's nature and destiny may shine in the heavens, but be denied on earth. And sadly enough, unless a true revolution occurs, future generations of historians may ask why our scientists and engineers did not really join the human race in our times, when the opportunities were so great, the means at hand so magnificent, but so badly used despite those who most desperately needed our help to realize what we profess to be man's exalted nature and destiny.

SCIENTIFIC STATESMANSHIP [6]

BARRY COMMONER [7]

According to George H. T. Kimble of Indiana University, on the North American continent alone "at least 10,000 communities, representing a population of more than 100 million, are now seriously affected by [air] pollution." This is a dramatic reminder, as Dr. Kimble reports, that we live "in the midst of dirty air . . . air that we ourselves have dirtied." And the enormity of the problem is pointed up, particularly when we remember that the toxicity of the air caused by chemical fumes is but one aspect of the total danger of pollution. To this danger must be added the threats arising from radioactive fallout, and from the indiscriminate use of pesticides—a theme that provoked increasingly wide controversy following the publication of Rachel Carson's *Silent Spring* last year.

At a meeting of the National Conference on Air Pollution in Washington, D.C., on December 10, 1962, Barry Commoner, professor of plant physiology at Washington University, St. Louis, dealt candidly and perceptively with the hazards that often result from the impingement of scientific and technological advances upon the environment in which man lives. And he stressed the necessity of our discerning the proper roles "of scientific knowledge and social judgment" in making decisions regarding the proper use of the new developments:

> Certainly science can validly describe what is known about the information to be gained from a nuclear experiment, the economic value of a highway, or the hazard of radioactive contamination or of smog. The statement will usually be hedged with uncertainty, and the proper answer may sometimes be: "We don't know"; but in any case these separate questions do belong within the realm of science. However, the choice of the balance point between benefit and hazard is a value judgment; it is based on ideas of social good, on morality or religion— *not on science.*

Dr. Commoner proposed the organization "*in advance* of any large-scale technological innovation of an open *scientific inquiry* to consider the state of knowledge about the associated benefits and hazards":

> I believe, for example, that the scientific community might have done a great deal to mitigate the present conflicts about insecti-

[6] Text furnished by Dr. Commoner, with permission for this reprint. Full rights in the speech remain with Dr. Commoner.

[7] For biographical note, see Appendix.

cides, fallout and smog, if it had applied the customary principles of scientific inquiry to these problems *at the right time*.
Clearly, the decisive time to evaluate the risks associated with a
new technological program is *before it is put into effect*.

He warned, however, that "no amount of advance information will
suffice if it is not in the hands of those who must serve as the final
arbiters of social good—the citizens." And he believed this was possible,
provided "citizens accept the duty to learn, and scientists accept the
duty to teach."

That science should require the guidance of statesmanship
and statesmanship the discipline of science is a special mark
of these disjointed times. Science, which is at its source an encounter of a single mind with the stern reality of nature, would
appear to have no cause to weigh the wisdom of its inevitable
course. The affairs of state, which are guided by values that are
remote from natural law, have seemingly little need for the
discipline of science.

Why then have science and statesmanship become—as they
now are—so closely intertwined? Seventy years ago Pasteur could
advise students, "Whatever your career may be, do not let yourselves be discouraged by the sadness of certain hours that pass
over nations. Live in the serene peace of laboratories and li-
braries." Why has the serenity of the laboratories been swept
away by intruding social problems? Why has the discipline of
science now intervened in the councils of state? Where in this
tangled design lies the duty of the scientist to society, to science,
to himself?

The answer, I believe, lies in understanding the paradoxical
effects of scientific progress on the welfare of man. Nowhere is
this paradox more acutely revealed than in the problem of environmental pollution.

This conference is concerned with finding ways to free the air
of its growing burden of pollution. That such a conference should
be necessary at this time sharply illuminates the conflicting effects
of science on society.

We are living in a time of astonishing scientific progress.
Scientific research has become a powerful tool for analyzing the
natural world, from the depths of the earth to the outer reaches
of space. Evidence of its success—the wonderful harvest of technological applications—is all around us: space vehicles, nuclear

power, numerous new synthetic chemicals, great improvements in the practice of agriculture, medical advances which have significantly increased the length and usefulness of human life.

But we also see some sharp contrasts. At this moment, in some other city, a group may be meeting to consider how to provide air for the first human inhabitants of the moon. Yet, we are meeting here because we have not yet learned how to manage our lives without fouling the air that man must continue to breathe on mother earth. We hear of masterful schemes for using nuclear explosions to extract pure water from the moon; but in some American cities the water that flows from the tap is no longer an entirely palatable fluid, and the householder will find it instead in bottles on the market shelf. Science in 1962 is radiant with far-flung success, and—it would seem—clouded by growing difficulties in providing for the necessities of life.

Why should this be so? Is the pollution of the air that we breathe and of the water that we drink only a passing imperfection in human society? Or is it a more serious matter—a warning that despite all the new powers of science, or perhaps because of them, we can no longer exert a sufficient mastery of our environment?

Air pollution is only one of a number of new and unwelcome problems: the pollution of water, not only by human waste, but by synthetic chemicals; unwonted loss of animals and plants, and possible health hazards from widespread dissemination of pesticides and herbicides; confusion about tolerable levels of chemical food additives; the hazards of radioactive wastes from nuclear reactors and of fallout from nuclear explosions.

These problems have in common a set of relationships to science, and a troublesome involvement in public controversy.

1. Each of these difficulties is a result of scientific and technological progress. The new synthetic chemicals, which are the fruits of remarkable advances in chemical technology since World War II appear in a multitude of useful forms—but also as pollutants of air and water. The development, just twenty years ago, of self-sustained nuclear reactions has given us not only new weapons and sources of power—but radioactive debris as well.

2. Many of these problems seem to crop up unexpectedly. The photochemical conversion of hydrocarbons, which produces

smog, was discovered not in a chemical laboratory but in the air over Los Angeles, long after the technological practices that disseminated the hydrocarbons were well entrenched in our economic life. The resistance of synthetic detergents to bacterial degradation was apparently discovered only when the resultant accumulation in water supplies became noticeable, by which time detergents were already a common household item. The absorption of certain radioisotopes in the human body became known only some years after the establishment of massive programs of nuclear testing. All of these problems have been imposed on us—sometimes with a considerable surprise—well after the causative activity was in full swing.

3. It is also characteristic of the pollution problem—whether of air, water or food—that the most serious difficulties arise in the realm of biology. Unfortunately, the processes which are the biological targets of modern pollutants are singularly intractable to scientific analysis. The hazards from certain air pollutants and from radioactive wastes are due to the possibility that they may induce cancers. The origin of cancerous growth and the mode of action of chemicals and radiation in promoting it, remain, of course, one of the great unsolved problems of modern science. The mechanism of action of DDT on insects, or its effects in mammals are poorly understood. Despite very considerable investigation the basic mechanism of plant growth, with which the new synthetic herbicides interact, remains unknown.

There is, then, a remarkable incongruity between the two ways in which science enters into modern pollution problems. On the one hand scientific research has produced chemical and radioactive pollutants hitherto absent from the surface of the earth. But at the same time modern science appears to be poorly prepared to understand the particular biological damage that these new materials may cause.

The recent history of the sciences reveals some of the reasons for these conflicting consequences of scientific progress. Nuclear technology results from laboratory experiments on fission reactions first reported some thirty years ago; and behind this discovery lay the great revolution in our basic understanding of the structure of matter which took place at the turn of the century. One reason for the remarkable growth in the number of synthetic organic chemicals is that chemical engineering, which was once an empirical technology has now become firmly based on the theoretical knowledge of the mechanisms of chemical reactions—which is in turn elucidated by the new physical theories.

While physics and chemistry and its technological offshoots have been radically reformed by the theoretical revolution that began about fifty years ago, biology—or at least those areas related to the effects of the new pollutants—has proven to be considerably more resistant to change. Anyone who wishes to be convinced of this, need only compare the present textbooks of physics, chemistry and biology with those of, let us say, twenty-five years ago. A twenty-five-year-old text in organic chemistry is a densely packed summary of empirical knowledge about a vast array of organic reactions; but the modern text is a logically organized consideration of the electronic structures of atoms and molecules, and describes how this knowledge can guide the chemist in controlling reactions and in synthesizing new molecules to specification. On the other hand, current textbook discussions of the physiology of plant growth, or of the mechanism of carcinogenesis, while they may be couched in the language of present fads in experimentation lead to the same final answer offered by a twenty-five-year-old text: The mechanism of growth, whether of plants or of neoplasms, remains unknown.

If basic theories of physics had not attained their present power we would not be confronted with massive dissemination of man-made radioactive isotopes and synthetic chemicals. If biological theory had by now become sufficiently advanced to master the problems of normal and neoplastic growth we might be better prepared to cope with these modern pollutants. We are in difficulty because of a wide disparity between the present state of the physical and biological sciences.

Trouble arises because the separation of the laws of nature among the different sciences, is, of course, a human conceit; nature itself is an integrated whole. We classify nuclear explosions as experiments in physics, representing a step in a progression of growing knowledge about nuclear reactions. Yet every nuclear explosion is also a vast experiment in biology, but one which is only remotely connected with earlier biological research. Thus, modern physics was ready to detect strontium 90, to analyze its nuclear structure and to understand its origin in the fission reaction. In contrast, modern biology was quite unprepared for the entry of strontium 90 on the scene, for until the fallout problem revealed the necessity for such studies, *normal* strontium metabolism was an almost completely neglected subject.

The same pattern can be found in most of our pollution problems. The development of highly efficient new insecticides reflects an impressive mastery of chemical synthesis and of methods of dissemination. But the intrusion of a new insecticide into the biosphere may lead to rude surprises.

The current debate about insecticides reminds me of my own education in this matter. During World War II, I served as project officer in the Navy's development of aircraft dispersal of DDT—which proved to be of great importance in the Pacific battles. The project made meticulous studies of aerosol production, aerodynamic distribution, insect kill, meteorological effects, and problems of flying tactics. Toward the end of our work, when we were justifiably proud of a system ready for fleet operations, we received a request for help from an experimental rocket station on a strip of island beach off the New Jersey coast. Urgent experimental work was severely hampered by flies; would the Navy please get rid of them. We doused the island with DDT. Within half a day the beach became a flyless paradise and the rocketeers went about their work with renewed vigor. But a week later they were on the telephone again. A mysterious epidemic had littered their beach with tons of decaying fish—and all the flies in New Jersey had come to enjoy the fun. This is how I learned that DDT kills fish.

I believe that the history of modern pollution problems shows that most of them result from the same general fault. We have been massively intervening in the natural world, without being aware of many of the biological consequences until the act has been performed, and its effects—which are difficult to understand, and sometimes irreversible—are upon us. We can produce and widely disseminate radioisotopes, but do not fully comprehend how they will affect life. We can synthesize and disseminate a marvelous variety of synthetic chemicals before we have sufficiently mastered what they will do in a living organism. Like the sorcerer's apprentice, our education is dangerously incomplete.

It will be argued, I know, that this is nothing new—that it is the grand purpose of science to move into unknown territory, to explore and to discover. It can be said that similar risks have been taken before, and that science and technology cannot move forward without taking some risks.

But these arguments overlook an important element which *is new*. In the past, the risks taken in the name of scientific progress—boiler explosions on the first riverboats, or the early experiments with X-rays—were restricted to a small place and a brief time. But the processes which we now strive to master are neither local nor brief in their effects. Air pollution covers vast urban areas. Fallout is world-wide. Synthetic chemicals may remain in the soil for years. Radioactive pollutants now in the biosphere will be found there for generations, and in the case of carbon 14 for thousands of years. The size and persistence of possible errors has grown with the expanding power of modern science.

One can also argue that the hazards of modern pollutants are small compared to the dangers associated with other human enterprises—such as automotive traffic. But no estimate of the actual harm that may be done by smog, fallout or chemical residues can obscure the sober realization that the risk was taken before it was fully understood. The importance of these issues to science lies not so much in the technical difficulty of estimating the associated hazards, but in that they warn of an incipient abdication of one of the major duties of science—prediction and control of human interventions into nature. The true measure of the danger is not represented by the present hazard, but by the disasters that will surely be visited upon us if we dare to enter the new age of science that lies before us without repairing this basic fault in the scientific enterprise.

Having examined some of the scientific difficulties associated with modern pollution, what can be said about the scientist's relationship to the social problems that follow in their wake? Each of the issues that I have mentioned has been marked by public confusion and controversy, severe legislative debate and enormous administrative difficulties. They represent a veritable jungle in which science, industry, economics, local politics, foreign affairs, religion and morality intermix in uproarious confusion. No scientist who enjoys the quiet of his laboratory or the reasonableness and objectivity of scientific discourse, is likely to walk into this wilderness voluntarily—or to emerge from it unscathed.

That thousands of scientists—including those present at this conference—have been willing to devote their skill and energy to bring order out of this chaos reflects, I believe, the serious impact which these problems have had on the inner life of science.

In no area has there been a more serious concentration of effort than in the problem of low-level radiation from fallout, particularly under the aegis of the United States Public Health Service. The recent history of this issue provides a clear picture of how the social problems emerge from scientific ones and can illuminate some general aspects of environmental pollution as a whole.

Until a few years ago the possible effects of low-level radiation were guided by the assumption that doses below a particular level would cause no discernible medical effects. Since the estimation of the threshold dose is a purely scientific matter it was possible for groups of scientists, such as the International Committee for Radiation Protection, to deliberate on the problem and recommend some permissible level of radiation which ought not to be exceeded if medical hazard is to be avoided.

However, evidence has since accumulated which suggests that one cannot safely assume any threshold in the relationship between radiation dosage and the resultant biological effects. Consequently, beginning in 1958 scientific agencies charged with the responsibility of setting radiation protection standards uniformly adopted the assumption that any increment in radiation exposure, however slight, is accompanied by a comparable increase in the risk of medically undesirable effects. If this is the case, and there is no *absolutely* safe limit, how can one determine what dosage is to be tolerated?

This judgment requires a balance between the risk associated with a given dosage and some possibly countervailing benefit. The agency now responsible for setting radiation standards in the United States, the Federal Radiation Council, has explicitly stated this position.

If . . . beneficial uses were fully exploited without regard to radiation protection, the resulting biological risk might well be considered too great. Reducing the risk to zero would virtually eliminate any radiation use, and result in the loss of all possible benefits. It is therefore necessary to strike some balance between maximum use and zero risk. In establishing radiation protection standards, the balancing of risk and benefit is a decision involving medical, social, economic, political and other factors. Such a balance cannot be made on the basis of a precise mathematical formula but must be a matter of informed judgment. [Report No. 1, May 13, 1960.]

This approach is, I believe, equally applicable to most other pollution problems. Since they are all large-scale effects and influence a wide variety of living organisms, on statistical grounds alone, it is probable that the smallest detectable pollutant level represents some hazard, however slight, and that the risk will increase roughly with the level.

What is the proper role of the scientists in such a judgment? What *scientific* procedure can determine, for example, whether the benefits to the national interest of nuclear testing outweigh the hazards of fallout? What is the "importance" of fallout, determined scientifically? Some scientists have stated, with the full dignity of their scientific pre-eminence, that the fallout hazard while not zero is "trivial." Nevertheless I have seen a minister upon learning for the first time that acts deliberately performed by his own nation were possibly endangering a few lives in distant lands and a future time, become so incensed at this violation of the biblical injunction against the poisoning of wells, as to make an immediate determination to oppose nuclear testing. What science can gauge the relative validity of these conflicting responses to the same facts?

How can scientific method determine whether the proponents of urban superhighways or those who complain about the resultant smog are in the right? What scientific principle can tell us how to make the choice—forced upon us by the insecticide problem—between the shade of the elm tree and the song of the robin?

Stated in this form, the answer to these questions becomes apparent. Certainly science can validly describe what is known about the information to be gained from a nuclear experiment, the economic value of a highway, or the hazard of radioactive contamination or of smog. The statement will usually be hedged with uncertainty, and the proper answer may sometimes be: "We don't know"; but in any case these separate questions do belong within the realm of science. However, the choice of the balance point between benefit and hazard is a value judgment; it is based on ideas of social good, on morality or religion— *not on science.*

There can be no scientific agreement on such judgments; answers will differ according to religious or political outlook. Scientists who present their own judgments on these matters as though they *were* scientific evaluations are simply forcing a disagreement which can never be resolved by scientific means. Such a disagreement appears as a perplexing exception to scientists' vaunted skill at winning truth. The citizen will be driven to ask a question which is now heard with increasing frequency, "How do we know which scientist is telling the truth?" This doubt can only impair confidence in the validity of the excellent methods which science possesses for getting at the truth—about scientific questions.

In the "informed judgment" of which the Federal Radiation Council so properly speaks, the scientist can justly claim to be "informed," but in my opinion he can make no valid claim for a special competence in "judgment." To act otherwise, is to corrupt the meaning of science and to undermine its usefulness to society.

I believe that once the scientific evidence has been stated, or its absence made clear, the establishment of a level of tolerance for a modern pollutant is a *social* problem and must be resolved by social processes. In these processes the scientist has one vote and no claim to leadership beyond that given to *any* person who has the gift of moving his fellow men. But the government official, whose task is to make these judgments, and the citizen— who must provide the social ideology which guides administrative decision—require for these purposes the necessary facts and the relevant evaluations. Where these are matters of science, the scientist as the custodian of this knowledge has a profound duty to impart as much of it as he can to his fellow citizens. But in doing so he must guard against false pretensions, and avoid claiming for science that which belongs to the conscience.

In this discussion I have tried to show that the scientific and social difficulties that encumber the problems of modern pollution reflect a basic flaw in the present relations between science and social processes. We have not yet learned how to apply modern science in a manner which is consistent with its enormous power and its present inadequacies. We have not yet learned to discern in these complex problems, the proper roles of scientific knowledge and social judgment.

It seems to me that until effective means for dealing with these questions are developed we will be in continuous danger from unanticipated and poorly understood hazards, which will grow in magnitude as the power of science advances. If we are to live securely with the new discoveries and inventions of modern science, we shall need as well new inventions to govern the relation between science and society.

Although the task of developing such new procedures is formidable, there are some useful guidelines in our recent experience. I believe, for example, that the scientific community might have done a great deal to mitigate the present conflicts about insecticides, fallout and smog, if it had applied the customary principles of scientific inquiry to these problems *at the right time.* Clearly, the decisive time to evaluate the risks associated with a new technological program is *before* it is put into effect. The longer such an evaluation is delayed, the less its value to society, for once the process has become embedded in a vast economic or political commitment, it may be nearly impossible to alter.

In this task, the scientist's duty is plain, for it is no different from his responsibilities toward the development of all scientific knowledge. The scientist must examine all the evidence and summarize it in a statement of what is known, what is assumed, what is doubtful, and what is possibly erroneous. He must also describe the limits of the relevant knowledge, for these will reveal what new knowledge is needed and indicate when a proposed technological application may expose us to the dangers of acting in ignorance.

I make this proposal quite conscious of the obstacles which may block scientific evaluation of risks and benefits *in advance* of a proposed technological innovation. Perhaps the most serious of these is that the Government's military or political necessities, or an industry's competitive position may dictate secrecy. A recent scholarly review of the toxicology of herbicides, written to enlighten the scientific community and to encourage new work on this difficult problem states in its opening paragraph:

Many of the toxicological data underlying assessment of the risks involved by using them [weed killers] in practice originate from confidential, nonpublished reports placed at the disposal of the authorities concerned. Such data have not been included in the present survey. [Dalgaard-Mikkelsen and Poulsen, *Pharmacological Reviews,* v. 14, no. 2. Je. '62.]

We pay a steep price for this kind of secrecy. Scientific knowledge is not created whole in one man's mind, or even in the deliberations of a committee. Each separate scientific analysis yields an approximate result and inevitably contains some errors and omissions. Science gets at the truth by a continuous process of self-correction, which remedies omissions and corrects errors. In this process, the key elements are open disclosure of results, their general dissemination in the community of scientists and the resultant verification, criticism and correction. Anything that blocks this process will hamper the approach to the truth. The basic difficulty with secrecy in science is that mistakes made in secret will persist. Every attempt to keep a scientific problem secret is paid for in the most expensive currency in the world—knowledge.

Science has great power to serve society. But it cannot properly perform this function if deprived of access to the facts. The time has come, I believe, for Government and industry alike to consider with great care the relative benefits and risks associated with the avoidance of full and early disclosure of scientific evidence relevant to large scale processes that may result in environmental pollution. I believe that the present confusion and controversy about these problems is part of the price paid for secrecy, and in my opinion the price is uneconomical for both industry and the nation.

It should be possible, I believe, to find ways of bringing the full force of scientific knowledge—which is something that only the total community of scientists possesses—to bear on these problems. An important first step might be the organization, *in advance* of any large-scale technological innovation of an open *scientific inquiry* to consider the state of knowledge about the associated benefits and hazards. This, or any other, procedure must be established soon, for new proposals are being advanced constantly. Suggestions have been made for the use of mutagenic (and therefore also carcinogenic) chemicals for controlling insects by inducing sterilization. This may entail new biological hazards. Surely the scientific community can arrange to discuss these openly and widely *before* the proposal is put into effect.

If we develop such new means for orderly consideration of the problems of environmental pollution they will have a much wider usefulness. Consider, for example, a proposal which is about to be considered by the Government to develop airliners designed to fly at two or three times the speed of sound. Such an airliner flying across the United States will produce in a zone twenty-five miles wide a continuous series of intense sonic booms. Where in our social processes have we weighed whatever benefit is involved in traveling from coast to coast in two hours against the hazards associated with the effects of sonic booms?

I can report that in my own city the resolution of this balance has taken a rather curious form. For a period of weeks earlier this year St. Louis endured sonic booms sometimes at hourly intervals and often in the small hours of the night. The hazards were clear: The Air Force was besieged with claims for broken windows, cracked walls and fallen ceilings. Citizens complained about children awakened or frightened while awake. Protests began to mount, but not enough to counterbalance the military benefits of the flights—for they continued. I offer as a possibly useful piece of evidence regarding the weight to be accorded such benefits and hazards that when two gazelles in the St. Louis Zoo became so startled one night as to die in the ensuing upset— the flights were abruptly halted.

Is this the proper measure of the sonic boom hazard? Do we know enough about the number of babies that will be awakened every night by a supersonic airliner to make an "informed judgment" on its social usefulness? Do we really understand the physiological effects of the rather sudden compression associated with a sonic boom to be capable of evaluating the basic medical hazard? If these factors are not yet understood how can a Government agency, or the citizen, make the necessary informed judgment? If we invest nearly $1 billion in an airliner before we have determined whether its social usefulness will outweigh its social harm, will the step become thereby an irreversible one? Surely we need a scientific inquiry into this project before it is committed to action.

But no amount of advance information will suffice if it is not in the hands of those who must serve as the final arbiters of social good—the citizens. Can this be done? Can we expect our citizens to comprehend the benefits and hazards of nuclear reactions? Can they understand the relationship between hydrocarbons, sunlight and smog?

I am convinced that this is possible—providing citizens accept the duty to learn, and scientists accept the duty to teach. The task will not be an easy one, but I believe that we have the resources at hand. This vast educational task is not one that ought to be delegated alone to those scientists who have already devoted their professional energies to the problems of environmental pollution. These problems are so large and range so widely across the spectrum of science, that *all* scientists, regardless of their immediate professional interest are intimately concerned with them. Pollution of the environment touches the work of every meteorologist, ecologist, or chemist; the possible hazards are of interest to every biochemist and to every specialist in the biological and medical sciences.

Knowledge of these problems, and the willingness to explain them to the public, should, I believe, be the responsibility of each of the more than 100,000 scientists of this nation. Given this army of teachers, which is available to almost every community in the country, this educational task can surely be accomplished. Already in a number of cities, groups of scientists are educating their fellow citizens about radiation problems; I believe that given adequate support and the broad participation of all scientists, such groups should be capable of expanding their work to encompass the broad range of problems of environmental pollution.

Nor should we be discouraged by the difficulties and disagreements that now burden these problems. The attention which these controversies generate can serve as a timely warning that we must learn—now, before the hazards of unwitting action overtake us—how to live in the new world that science is creating. Science has placed enormous new powers at the hand of man. If we accept with these powers, the new responsibilities which must govern their use, science can serve its true goal—the welfare of man.

THE PROSPECT FOR CIVILIZATION [8]

Francis H. Horn [9]

In an age which offers ready evidence for the preparation of testaments of despair, it is heartening but not a little surprising, perhaps, to find an affirmation of faith in the future of the human race. Such is the thesis, however, of Francis H. Horn, president of the University of Rhode Island, in a confidently optimistic address delivered at the midwinter convocation at Ricker College, Houlton, Maine, on February 15, 1963. Dr. Horn does not minimize today's hazards and lethal threats; but he believes that man has the necessary resources of intellect and conscience to insure the survival of civilization.

Dr. Horn's speech offers a theme which students may wish to explore in talks and essays, their own and others'. Does the possibility of atomic destruction make previous predictions about man's increasing mastery of nature and himself sound a trifle hollow? Can we properly find solace in the traditional hopes, now that extinction is a conceivable result of war? Writing during the dark days of 1939, Irwin Edman, in his poetically haunting *Candle in the Dark*, reminded us that "this is not the first time in history . . . that the good and the reasonable saw nothing to do but to die or to shudder. . . . Men in earlier ages, too, thought they were living at the end of the world." He urged his readers to keep the arts and intellectual activities alive, despite momentary despair, so that civilized interests might not lapse. This is a familiar and laudable theme, also voiced impressively by Monroe E. Deutsch in a speech published in REPRESENTATIVE AMERICAN SPEECHES: 1942-1943. We should remember, said Mr. Deutsch, "that time is longer than the years of a war, however many they may be. And while wars go on, men and women perform deeds that last long after the din of battle has ceased." But today's despair, if indeed such it may be called, unquestionably has a new dimension.

Several weeks ago I received a letter from the Ford Foundation's Fund for the Republic which said: "The world has just witnessed historic events that could have ended our civilization had not reason prevailed. [It referred to the Cuban crisis.] Mankind was saved. But can we count on such good fortune at the next confrontation of naked power and overstrained nerves? This

---

[8] Text furnished by Dr. Horn, with permission for this reprint.

[9] For biographical note, see Appendix.

is the overwhelming concern of every thinking person in our society today."

I wish to direct your attention to this problem of the prospect for civilization. Let me emphasize that I am not an expert on this subject. I am not a historian or a political scientist. I come to you as a "thinking person," to whom, as the Fund's letter states, this matter of survival and the kind of a world tomorrow will bring is the "overwhelming concern."

In considering the future for mankind, I shall endeavor to make a case that though the world is teetering on the edge of an abyss, it will not only not tumble into it, but indeed move forward to the greatest future man has ever known.

Man's achievements, especially in science and technology, have brought the world, the Western world in particular, to the highest standards of living in history. The challenge is to extend this condition to people everywhere in the world, and in the process to eliminate the hunger, disease, and ignorance that have plagued man since the beginning of time. The attainment of this goal, however, is hampered by problems which the advances of science and technology have created, or at least aggravated.

Three major problems stand in the way of a better world for all peoples. The first is that of diminishing resources in the light of the so-called "population explosion." Science is overcoming famine, though not hunger, and disease. Infant mortality is declining and man is living longer. Surviving to 100 may well become normal; doctors have predicted that in time the life span may even reach 140 to 150 years. Already the result is a vast increase in the world's population. And UNESCO estimates that the present 3 billion will exceed 6 billion by the year 2000. Julian Huxley has predicted that it may reach 40 billion. A demographer on our faculty has indicated that in 200 years, United States population alone could exceed 200 billion, and in 400 years, be increasing at the rate of a billion a year. The late Sir Charles Darwin has made the dire prediction that in 1,000 years there will be standing room only on the earth. He is pessimistic about efforts to control population, especially in such countries as India and Japan. "All known methods of reducing world population are not likely to succeed," he declared.

The task of feeding, clothing, housing, and employing this rapidly growing population staggers the imagination. Resources can't keep pace with this growth, even with all the scientific know-how at our command. The problem is aggravated by the ways in which science is upsetting the balance of nature. The result, according to Darwin, is that "each year, the world's population has less food per person than the year before. In the end, sometime after the next two generations, mankind will run out of food and space and be forced back on 'survival of the fittest.' " This may seem incredible to us Americans, whose problem is food surpluses and to whom the land available seems inexhaustible. But students of the world-wide problem are not optimistic about a solution.

The second major cloud obscuring the hope for civilization is ethnic, racial, and religious prejudice. This problem has existed since the dawn of history, but modern science, especially as it affects mobility and communication, intensifies the dangers. Today, this conflict is most apparent in the relationships between black men and white men. The situation is most dangerous in Africa, but it is just as real here in the United States, where our treatment of the Negro is the most vulnerable crack in the armor of our democratic tradition and philosophy. The problem is not confined to the deep South; it exists right here in New England, where in my state, for example, Negroes are often denied not only equality of opportunity in housing, and employment, but even the common decencies of service in barbershops and restaurants.

Religious conflict, intensified by nationalism, still threatens the hope for civilization. In our day we have seen the massacre of millions of Hindus and Moslems that attended the agony of the separation of Pakistan and India; the continuing bitter hatred of Arab and Jew in the Near East; the conflict of Moslem and Christian in the Algerian struggle for independence. One would have thought that man would have long since got over killing his fellow man because of the color of his skin, his religious belief, or who his ancestors were. Though today in America we seldom shed blood over such differences, these prejudices remain and are a strain on our democratic society. Here and everywhere, these problems stand in the way of the better world for all peoples that lies within our grasp.

The third and at present the most crucial problem clouding the future for mankind is war and the threat of war. Since the end of World War II, we have lived in a divided world against

a background of the cold war, which intermittently becomes
painfully hot. Trouble spots erupt all over the world; some develop into little wars, brush-fire wars, fought on conventional
lines. The worry is that these will develop into big wars, fought
with nuclear bombs. As a result of living with the cold war, we
are becoming conditioned to the inevitability of war. Berlin is
perhaps the key to our thinking about war. Norman Cousins has
remarked:

> We know, for example, as Americans, that our nation cannot turn
> away from Berlin. The lines are drawn and the commitments made.
> The major powers are prepared to fight for West Berlin, but we know
> that fighting will not save it, any more than any city, whether Berlin
> or London or Moscow or New York, can be saved when the big bombs
> start to fall.

Yet we keep on working on these big bombs. Our current
budget for military spending is over $50 billion, half of the total
Federal budget. This is the appropriation for *defense*—an interesting term, since there is no real defense once the big bombs are
loosed. The purpose of these vast sums is to insure the security
of the nation, when there is no real security, and indeed with
each new and bigger bomb there is less security.

Scientists are at work on ever greater instruments of destruction, the asteroid bomb, for example—a "continent-shattering
weapon produced by diverting a tiny planet from its orbit so it
would strike the earth"—and a new hydrogen bomb with destructive power one thousand times greater than that of our present
multimegaton bombs. The neutrons from the latter's blast would
blanket a 200,000-square-mile area, in which all vegetable and
animal life would die, including people in the average basement
shelter. While scientists are working on ever more deadly bombs,
other scientists are working on frightening biological and chemical killers.

It is obvious that whereas the conditions and causes that lead
to disputes have not changed, the means of settling them by war
have changed. For the first time, man has the power to destroy
the civilization he has so painstakingly built up over the centuries, to wipe from the globe the great achievements of his hands
and brain and creative spirit.

If the catastrophe should come, man will not disappear from
the earth. In some place, some men will survive, as Carl Sand-

burg has pointed out in one of his latest poems. But most survivors will face conditions that have no appeal to rational man. As Nobel Prize biologist Dr. Albert Szent-Györgyi pointed out in warning that we are on our way to doomsday, any survivors of an atomic war will form "a primitive, barbaric society."

Even if we avoid the actual war, the danger for man from the testing of atomic weapons in the atmosphere is great. Certainly the genetic material which carries the future of the human race would be damaged. How much damage is a matter of controversy, but I am willing to side with those scientists who warn against the increasing dangers of radiation.

There is another danger to civilization even if war is avoided. In our fear of war and of the Communists whom we regard as threatening our liberties, we may accept a tightening of controls over our basic freedoms, and end up with an authoritarian society under a totalitarian government in which the very liberties we are planning to preserve are lost. The enslavement of mankind such as is envisaged in Huxley's *Brave New World* or Orwell's *1984*, is scarcely an acceptable alternative to utter annihilation.

Against these threats to civilization—diminishing resources in the face of a population explosion; racial, ethnic, and religious prejudices; and war—what resources does man have at his disposal? He has first of all, science. Yet the very successes of science, as I have pointed out, have created new problems or aggravated the age-old ones.

Man also has at his command the resource of language. As the world has shrunk in size, and communication around the globe become almost instantaneous, the role of language in reaching understanding between peoples becomes more and more significant. Dr. Mario Pei has long advocated one language for the world. It seems like the pipe-dream of an impractical professor. So did a trip to the moon not so long ago. Certainly, as communication among peoples improves, the chance for the survival of civilization likewise improves.

Another of the resources in man's battle for survival is his creative spirit as evidenced in great art, architecture, music, and literature—the manifestations of beauty in all its forms. The fine arts and literature, like mathematics and science, are universal in appeal and acceptance. They know no national boundaries. They may be counted on not only to enrich men's lives, but also, particularly through programs of cultural exchange, to create conditions in which it becomes more difficult to blow up the world and end civilization.

Most important of all the resources by which man may create a world of peace, a world closer to his heart's desire, in which each individual may fulfill himself, is the human mind. The potential of the human mind, through the use of reason, is practically limitless. Recall the remarkable achievements of this delicate instrument since Einstein first propounded his theory of relativity a half century ago. The humanist would hold that given time, and the will, man can ultimately solve all his problems and bring about the millennium he has longed for over the centuries. The humanist shares the optimistic view expressed by Professor Kermit Eby of the University of Chicago, that "we would like to believe that man is rational and humane and can achieve his ends by rational and humane means." But then, Eby goes on to say, "I look around, read the newspaper, listen to the radio, and my faith sinks. On every page, in every voice, there are announcements of violence, of death."

There are those, who seeing man's aberrations from the life of reason, hold that the human mind alone is not enough to avert catastrophe. Admittedly, human nature is imperfect, but this simply underlines the importance of developing and depending upon man's rational powers. We know that these can be trained, that men can learn to think more rationally, and, more important, to act more intelligently on the basis of rational thinking. As we bring more and more reason into the affairs of men and of nations, the prospect for civilization becomes less dim and gloomy than it may presently seem. The issue, it must be emphasized, is not merely the survival of civilization, but also the nature of the civilization that survives.

The question of what hope is there for civilization has four possible answers. First, there is no hope at all: sooner or later civilization will be destroyed by an all-out nuclear war and mankind and his works largely eliminated from the earth. Second, civilization will survive, but under very unsavory conditions. Most of mankind will live in constant fear of "the bomb," increasingly man will live underground, and he may be subjected to some form of totalitarianism that will make life grim, if not actually unbearable. Third, civilization will continue with life much as it is lived today. In the United States and Western nations, this life, with all its frustrations, tensions, and inequalities, is a pretty good one, better than the mass of mankind has ever lived before. It will be progressively extended to the rest of the world which now does not enjoy such a standard of living. Fourth and finally, there is a possibility of the life man has dreamt about for many centuries, a life in which the age-old scourges of famine, hunger, and disease are no more, where peace and brotherhood prevail—in short, a world in which is realized the old Chinese proverb that "under the heavens there is one family; within the four seas all men are brothers." This would be a world in which there is a genuine opportunity for each individual to fulfill himself, without regard to such matters as the color of his skin, the nature of his religious beliefs, the origin of his ancestors, or indeed, the kind of plumbing that he uses or of the food that he cooks.

Which of these possibilities seems most likely to prevail?

Certainly there is good reason for one to be pessimistic. Cuba brought us to the brink of war and remains a source of danger. The cold war is still very much with us. Military appropriations continue to increase. We are working on more deadly instruments of destruction. Atomic testing has been resumed. Disarmament efforts have failed. Other nations are endeavoring to produce nuclear bombs, especially France and China, and the latter nation has indicated it would not hesitate to use them. The dangers of this mad race were pointed out by Adlai Stevenson a year ago:

Every month that goes by without restriction on the testing, production, and transfer of nuclear weapons brings closer the moment when the genie will escape from the bottle. When a dozen or more states have their fingers on nuclear triggers, the possibility of their irresponsible release by someone, somewhere, will be multiplied. Does anyone doubt that Hitler would have unleashed all the Furies before he met his doom in the ruins of Berlin?

Those who would unleash a nuclear war are not just lunatics or fanatics. In 1962, General Walker in his testimony before Congress talked glibly of "opportunities we should have seized to go to war with the Russians." We apparently are still prepared to risk war over Cuba. There is, moreover, the terrible possibility of a war's being started by accident. A false alarm at

our base at Thule sent planes loaded with H-bombs to runways
at United States bases all around the world, ready to take off for
Russia. The recent novel *Fail-Safe* is built around what might
happen because of a mechanical breakdown in the controls governing our defense preparations.

With American troops and military power in many parts of
the world, with American fighting men dying in Southeast Asia,
we Americans are coming, as I have suggested in my comment
about Berlin, to accept the idea of war as inevitable. This change
in attitude is perhaps the greatest danger of all. Murray Lincoln,
board chairman of CARE, has written that "the forces that move
us toward war are getting stronger by the day . . . [and] a great
many people in this country are ready, in a resigned sort of way
for war—the war that only yesterday was unthinkable. You can
feel it in the conversations about bomb shelters, about stockpiling
food and water in the basement, about the morality of keeping
your neighbors away with a shotgun, about our ability to retaliate
and 'win!'"

Another dangerous factor is the growing power of the military
leadership in Washington and of the industrial might dependent
upon military spending. With more than $50 billion at stake,
with such plums up for grabs as the recently announced
$5 billion program of jet fighters, it is no wonder that the out-
come may be beyond control by people and by reason. President
Eisenhower, in one of his last press conferences, warned against
the growing influence of the military-industrial combination. If
its leaders determined that war with the Soviet Union were inevitable, they could make it so.

The outlook for avoiding a nuclear war looks dim, and yet,
I am not pessimistic. Not only do I not believe that such a war
is inevitable; I believe that it will be avoided and that civilization
will not be destroyed. What are the reasons for my optimism?
Let me suggest several.

First is Cuba. Regardless of the current controversy over the
extent of the Soviet power there, the Russians did back down and
war was avoided. The conflict with communism continues, but
Khrushchev is as anxious to avoid an all-out war as we are.
Ambassador Stevenson pointed out last year that peaceful coexistence was the cornerstone of Khrushchev's foreign policy.
"Whatever the ground rules of his coexistence game as he wishes

to play it, this appears to exclude the resort to nuclear war simply because the Soviet leader recognizes, as we do, its awful consequences." We are making some progress even in disarmament proposals, with Soviet concessions proffered on inspection. So long as we talk, we are not likely to drop the bombs.

President Kennedy has indicated our desire to cooperate with the U.S.S.R. in space science and exploration. Our cultural exchange program with the Soviets is increasing with beneficial results. On other fronts, we've had a cease-fire in Laos and the India-China war has ground to a halt. The Dutch New Guinea conflict did not explode into war, the bloody Algerian struggle for independence has terminated, and the United Nations seems to have ended the conflict in the Congo. Except for the Congo, incidentally, it must be remarked that in the last few years, dozens of new nations in Africa have come into being without bloodshed. None of them has fallen into the Communist camp and all seem to be placing special hope in the United Nations. True, fighting continues in parts of Southeast Asia, but if this were going to lead to a nuclear war, it would have already happened. No, I do not see such a war on the immediate horizon.

But what about the long-range hope for avoiding the war that will lead to Armageddon? Isn't Russia just stalling? Has Khrushchev not threatened to bury us? Aren't his plans for Communist domination of the world still uppermost in Soviet policy? Are we only postponing the day of reckoning?

I think not. Listen to Arnold Toynbee, who foresees the development of a common civilization:

If we manage to avoid fighting a third world war and therefore allow the human race to continue to exist, liberalism [Western democracy] and communism will be likely, bit by bit, to come closer to each other. There is one enormous leveling and unifying force which I personally find formidable and that is the force of technology. It is forcing all human beings all over the world into a common world, making over their social institutions and, more than that, their culture, their thoughts, their values. It is a thing that is going to diminish the differences between the two sides of the iron curtain.

This development, I believe, holds great hope for the future of civilization. But there are other concerns, in addition to the avoidance of a nuclear war, which demand man's attention, not only to enable civilization to survive, but also to move it forward toward the peaceful world people everywhere long for. Above all we must improve the lot of the great majority of the human race, the two thirds or three quarters of the people of the world who are neither Communists nor Western democrats.

These peoples need food and shelter, sanitation and roads, improved agriculture and industry, above all they need school-houses and schoolteachers. Both the material and spiritual stand-ards of these 2 billions of people must be raised. The task requires more of the energies and resources of the "have" nations, of the affluent societies. These people of the "have-not" nations now realize that they don't need to starve or see their children die of disease. They no longer will accept the conditions under which poor people have always lived, because they know they don't have to. It is not the will of God, but man's ways that have created their intolerable conditions.

We must work more positively to help them improve these conditions. At the moment we are only scratching the surface. The Peace Corps has been one new contribution to our efforts. Much more must be done, because there is little likelihood that in the long run our Western civilization will survive at its high level unless the standard of living everywhere in the world is progressively raised.

Another major concern that must occupy our attention and engage our best efforts, if civilization is to survive and prosper, is the creation of one world. Again, as the greatest historian of our time, Toynbee, has pointed out, intercontinental missiles have united the world as a common arena for warfare. Consequently, we will either destroy ourselves or learn to unify ourselves in a more spiritual sense by "creating one world, in which the whole human race can live together like a single family."

Progress toward one world will be difficult and long, especially in the United States, where Washington's admonition against entangling alliances is still used as an argument to defy the logic of geography and science in the space age. But the world, in-cluding the United States, is moving, quite rapidly in some respects, toward the inevitable goal. Who could have foreseen only a few years ago the progress toward a United States of Europe? The surprising thing about the French turndown of Britain for the Common Market is not General de Gaulle's posi-tion, but the bitterly unfavorable reaction by France's fellow members. The Atlantic Community and other regional groupings on the way toward one world are not just diplomatic agencies motivated by the age-old struggle for political power; they represent a new concept of togetherness, if you will, in a world made one by modern science in which, to adapt Benjamin Franklin's eighteenth century warning to the American colonies, all peoples must hang together or they will hang separately. People are recognizing the inevitability of giving up historic concepts of national sovereignty, of moving toward a government of law among nations. President Eisenhower said in 1958: "In a very real sense, the world no longer has a choice between force and law. If civilization is to survive, it must choose the rule of law."

The hope for civilization goes hand in hand with the movement toward a world legal order. We must begin by strengthening the one international organization that can develop into a focus for world law—the United Nations. The United Nations, Justice Warren has written, "can become the growing point of a true international system." The United Nations is not perfect— no agencies of man are—but it has survived some vicious attacks and is stronger than ever. The new nations of the world see it as a source of strength for them. The United States, as represented by both the Eisenhower and Kennedy administrations, is behind the United Nations even if the John Birchers and the DAR are not. In his second inaugural address, President Eisenhower declared: "We are pledged to honor, and to strive to fortify, the authority of the United Nations. For in that body rests the best hope of our age for the assertion of that law by which all nations may live in dignity."

World government must be our eventual goal, as Toynbee and many other distinguished citizens of the world suggest. All men of good will must work to strengthen the United Nations and its peace force. The United States and all other nations must put more of their resources, their energies, their talents, into the pursuit of peace and the building of the world community. Adlai Stevenson has stated that "for years many of us have been contending that if we would put into the service of peace even a small fraction of the scientific, technological, military, and political talent we lavish on war, the results might be dramatic." Norman Cousins has declared: "If the energy, money, and resources now going into [fallout] shelters were to be put to work

in the making of a better world, we would do far more to safeguard the American future than all the underground holes that
would be built in a thousand years."

Before long, even we Americans will realize this. We will
understand that there is hope for peace, and hence for civilization. In spite of the great obstacles that must be overcome, civilization is not going down the drain. Success won't come tomorrow, or perhaps in the lifetime of us now past fifty. But in the
lifetime of students now in school and college it will come.
Walter Lippmann has observed that "throughout Europe there is
a deep and ardent determination to overcome the obstacles [to
union and peace], if necessary, by outliving them." If we, too,
take the long view, we can find cause for optimism. Dean Gris-
wold of . . . [Harvard] Law School has pointed out that "*we*
should not forget that there were many centuries when men must
have looked at the plague and the smallpox, at slow communication and difficult transport, at heavy manual labor and household
drudgery with the same feeling of resignation and inevitability
with which they now sometimes regard the problems of crime
and civil controversy, or international relations and war."

Great progress has been accomplished in the areas of eliminating social injustice, for example, as in upgrading the position
of women and children. The most spectacular of achievements
of recent years has been the end of colonialism. Fifteen years ago,
Great Britain controlled an empire in Asia alone that contained
one sixth of the world's population. These peoples are now citizens of a number of independent states. In Africa, several dozen
new nations have emerged from the old ties of empire. The
world will go on making progress toward the better life for all
peoples that our knowledge and our skills make possible.

But this better world won't happen automatically. It cannot
be left to God, or to fate, or to chance. The better world will
occur only if we bring greater wisdom into the affairs of men
and of nations. Men are made wiser through education. Education, in the last analysis, therefore, is the key to the hope for
civilization, whether conceived in terms of mere survival or in
terms of the better world for all mankind that I have held out
as possible. It was H. G. Wells who half a century ago propheti-
cally declared that history become more and more a race between
education and catastrophe.

What are the goals of education, especially of higher education, that make it the key to the hope for civilization? First of all, our task is to remove ignorance and transmit knowledge. Knowledge, President Kennedy has written, "is the passkey to the future, . . . knowledge transcends national antagonisms, . . . speaks a universal language, . . . is a possession, not of a single class, a single nation, or a single ideology, but of all mankind."

Our second responsibility is to produce new knowledge, primarily through research. Today, thanks largely to the work of colleges and universities, knowledge in some fields is doubling every ten years. It is imperative that such an exploration of knowledge continue if we are to cope with the complex problems of our day.

Third, we must train manpower for the 1,001 specialized jobs needed by a technological society. Trained manpower is the most important commodity in today's world. Colleges don't make brains but if they do their job well, they develop the brains of their students to the maximum of their ability. The world needs such trained manpower as never before.

A special task is educating increasing numbers of such individuals for service in the developing nations. And, it must be emphasized, the need of the world is not just for trained scientists, engineers, and other technical specialists. The need is equally great for poets, artists, philosophers, and theologians.

Finally, and most important of all, is the task of developing, in the increasing numbers of students who are involved in our higher institutions, those qualities of rationality, of critical judgment, that are nurtured by a sound liberal education. I have stressed the need for greater wisdom in the affairs of men and of nations. This requires well-educated men and women everywhere in the world. Only with more and more of such individuals, can we lick the problems which cloud the future of civilization.

True education, it must be stressed, one which will enable its holder to make his maximum contribution to preserving, expanding, and improving our civilization, can come only with life-long learning. Continuing education beyond graduation from college and the completion of any post-baccalaureate professional or graduate education, is essential for today's world. In college, students lay the foundation for such life-long learning and cultivation of the mind. All students have an obligation to work to the maximum of their ability to achieve these goals of education.

I want to stress, moreover, that it is not enough just to develop one's intellectual powers. Brilliant and able minds are necessary to civilization; but by themselves they are not quite enough to save civilization and advance the welfare of mankind. For this the world needs men and women of virtue, dedication, and high moral integrity. There is little real hope for civilization unless, in addition to bringing greater knowledge into the affairs of men and of nations, we can establish higher standards of morality between individuals and between nations.

This emphasis brings me to my final point, addressed especially to college students. In the last analysis, the hope I have held out for civilization depends upon man—individual man. This is not fully appreciated by most people. They are overwhelmed by the vastness of the universe, with its billions of planets; by the time span of this earth of millions of years; by the huge mass of the world's population of 3 billion men, women, and children. All around them they see bigness—big labor, big government—all getting bigger and presumably more powerful. Above all, is the threat of annihilation that hangs over the world.

The result is apathy and resignation. We assume that there is little we can do as individuals in a world where the forces in control are so vast and so indifferent to the individual. At best, we acknowledge that our fate is in the hands of a few men wielding great power—the President, industrial tycoons, labor bosses, etc. I insist, however, that this viewpoint, if it prevails, holds more danger for civilization than the bomb itself.

Given men and women of reason, moral earnestness, and a drive for a better world, a better world is possible. Man is responsible in this day of the bomb, just as surely as he was in the day of the bow and arrow, for the directions of his own life, of the society of which he is a part, and of the course of history. Karl Jaspers in his volume *The Future of Mankind* writes: "No single person can control history, but each is responsible for trying to influence it creatively. This is true in spite of all the demonic forces in personal and social life which tend constantly to pervert or destroy man's freedom and reason."

I urge you students to believe that there is no cause to feel insignificant or helpless; it is wrong to be indifferent or apathetic because the world seems too vast, its problems too complex, for one individual to do anything important about them. The world of tomorrow will be what individuals today want it to be. It is we who make it—you and I and other individuals like us.

The prospect for civilization, therefore, is good if each of us develops our intellectual powers to the maximum and then uses reason based upon knowledge in tackling problems. In college, you must do your best to learn, not just facts, but those habits of thought and approaches to problems that mark the rational man.

But, again, intellectual capacity is not enough. You must commit yourself to high values. Your conduct must be governed by moral and spiritual considerations. Especially in these days, you must put concern for mankind over self-interest. If you and all of us do not, if we bow before the gods of materialistic self-interest, civilization is doomed just as surely as if someone pressed the button and released the missile or bomb that means nuclear war and ultimate destruction.

I have faith, particularly in young people, with whom I've worked as teacher and administrator for over thirty years. There is evidence on every hand that youth recognizes their responsibility for a better world; that they are accepting the challenge for service to society above self-interest. I believe that as new generations come along, dedicated to their own intellectual and moral best, the holocaust of war will be avoided and that slowly but surely mankind will move toward the longed-for world of true peace and universal brotherhood. The prospect for civilization, I am convinced, is a hopeful one.

SOME INQUIRIES INTO PERSISTENT THEMES

ADDRESS AT THE LOUIS MARSHALL AWARD DINNER [1]

Earl Warren [2]

Irwin Edman once remarked that "men must be in love with the good, if good is to be their habitual practice." This, in his view, meant more than merely "subscribing verbally to a set of moral ideals"; it required emotional commitment to ethical conduct as a way of life, and the *habitual* practice of it. This is a familiar theme: man's moral obligation and responsibility to himself and his fellow men. Few subjects are more complex, even if one goes along with the belief that man will react to the good if it is shown him.

Whether or not public morality is deteriorating, is arguable. Contrasted with practices of a hundred years ago, particularly at governmental levels, today's conduct doubtless reflects a more faithful devotion to high standards of public morality. But with increasing complexity of governmental, industrial, and professional activity; with the growing necessity of handling allocations and contracts of astronomical size, demands arise periodically for establishing workable codes of ethics and for tightening the regulations governing conflicts of interest. It will be recalled that the Eighty-seventh Congress passed a law setting up a conflict-of-interest code for the executive branch of Government. On January 16, 1963, Senator Jacob K. Javits, Republican of New York, speaking for himself and his fellow senator, Kenneth B. Keating, submitted a concurrent resolution for the creation of a similar code of ethics for the legislative branch. Such ethical guidelines are part of what Senator Eugene J. McCarthy, Democrat of Minnesota, considers a necessary program for eliminating from the environment "whatever pushes man toward evil or leads him into error, and whatever establishes or sustains conditions which encourage man to easy response in action that is morally objectionable and wrong." Thus, presumably, man can come nearer to obeying the injunction in *I Corinthians,* 4:2: "It is required in stewards that a man be found faithful."

On November 11, 1962, Earl Warren, Chief Justice of the United States, delivered a major address on the relationship between ethics and law. Speaking at the Louis Marshall Award dinner of the Jewish

---

[1] Text furnished by Chief Justice Warren, with permission for this reprint.

[2] For biographical note, see Appendix.

Theological Seminary of America in New York City, Justice Warren recommended the development of a profession of counselor in ethics.

> We need law to guide us in areas properly subject to it. We decide through legal procedures, legislative, executive and judicial, how we should conduct ourselves in the vast areas of life subject to the scrutiny and power of society. A father may decide how his inheritance is to be divided among his children, and the courts will generally enforce his will. But the courts cannot compel his children to love one another, or even to behave as though they did.

Society, Justice Warren remarked,

> would come to grief without ethics, which is unenforceable in the courts, and cannot be made part of law. If there were no sense of love in families, if there were no sense of loyalty, if friendship meant nothing, if we all, or any large proportion of us were motivated only by avarice and greed, society would collapse almost as completely as though it lacked law. Not only does law in civilized society presuppose ethical commitment; it presupposes the existence of a broad area of human conduct controlled only by ethical norms and not subject to law at all.

There is a "law beyond the law" as binding "as the law itself, although there is no human power to enforce it." "Is it fantastic to suggest," the Chief Justice inquired, "that there is an urgent need in our troubled times for the development of the profession of the counselor in ethics, having the same relation to interpersonal conduct, beyond the law, that the lawyer has to conduct that is subject to the review in the courts?" Such counselors would cooperate with businessmen, politicians, labor leaders, college administrators and others in weighing proposed actions against considerations of private and public good.

Students of public address will find Chief Justice Warren's thesis inviting and provocative. For additional insights into the broad problem of public morality, they might like to read Stephen K. Bailey's *Ethics and the Politician,* a short paper published by the Center for the Study of Democratic Institutions (1960); "What Has Happened To Our Morality?" a collection of observations by Allan Nevins, Bishop James A. Pike, Eric Hoffer, Millicent C. McIntosh, and Charles Frankel, in the New York *Times Magazine,* June 10, 1962; Paul Douglas' *Ethics in Government* (1953); the weekly series of fourteen articles entitled "Challenge to Morality" in the *Christian Science Monitor,* beginning with the issue of Friday, January 4, 1963; and *Ethics and Bigness,* edited by Harlan Cleveland and Harold D. Lasswell (1962).

In civilized life, law floats in a sea of ethics. Each is indispensable to civilization. Without law, we should be at the mercy of the least scrupulous; without ethics, law could not exist. Without ethical consciousness in most people, lawlessness would be rampant. Yet without law, civilization could not exist, for there are always people who in the conflict of human interest, ignore their responsibility to their fellow man.

From the beginning, men discovered, even before they could articulate the principle, that material goods are finite and the desire for them is infinite. This inevitably led to conflict. Sometimes, such conflict occurred within the family, or clan, or tribe. Cain murdered Abel for a slight so insignificant that the Bible does not even record it. He was subject to punishment, for he had killed his own brother. In primitive life, if he had slain the member of another family, or clan, or tribe (depending on the degree of civilization), he would not have been punished, and his deed would not have been considered wrong by his relatives or clansmen or tribesmen. Law and ethics, which in primitive life were identical, protected only those within a limited group. In general, they offered little protection to outsiders. If a member of a group killed an outsider, the outside group felt it its duty to avenge the murder. This was a matter of law. The principle of the blood feud was a recognized institution in the early history of mankind, and survived even in parts of pioneering America. A person who injured a member of an outside group, whether family, clan or tribe, subjected himself to punishment by one of its members. If he could not be located, some other member of his group might suffer in his stead. This was considered not wrong, but right, not illegal, but legal.

The principle of the blood feud has been resurrected in our own times by gangsters who take the law into their own hands. It was also resurrected by Hitler, who was a special sort of gangster, and would sometimes wipe out whole villages to avenge the death of a member of the "master race" at the hands of a villager who could not be located.

Ultimately, as tribes merged into nation-states, the principle that violence—also in times of peace—is punishable by law, has been accepted the world over by civilized communities. No longer does injury to one's fellow require or justify vengeance by a relative of the injured. It requires action by the district attorney, representing the public at large. The slaying or injuring of any person is considered an insult to the majesty of the state, and the state must do its best to suppress such a tendency, no matter how unworthy the victim, no matter how great the injury. From time to time, people, husbands and wives, have appealed to a so-called unwritten law, giving an injured spouse the right to take vengeance on the person breaking up a family; but this exception, while eliciting sympathy, has no justification in the law of the land, or indeed in ethics. Wrongs, no matter how grave, have their remedy in the courts, if they are sufficiently serious and sufficiently clear. If they cannot be proven to the satisfaction of an impartial judge or jury, they cannot be punished either by the community or by the individual who considers himself wronged.

The ship of state, represented by the law, would begin to leak, and ultimately sink, if it permitted taking the law into one's own hands and obeying what one considered a moral command to avenge injustice to his brother. Where law asserts its authority, ethics must accept its dictates. It cannot be right, any more than it is legal, to lynch a person without trial, to steal from a thief, to return injury for injury.

On the other hand, without ethical understanding, the law, as a ship of state, would be stranded on dry land. Where there is no ethical commitment to observe the law, the judicial and police systems are really helpless, and law often ceases to operate at all. Therefore, the genius of the civilized world, particularly of the English-speaking peoples, has made obedience to law and acceptance of decisions of duly authorized agents of the community, whether legislative or juridical, mandatory as an ethical principle. This principle applies alike to majority and minority interests and groups.

Men defeated for office, frequently by a small margin of votes, accept the decision of the electorate as binding on them. Even when they consider such decisions perilous to the community, they do not pit their judgment against the majority, knowing full well that no danger to the state can be as great as the danger of lawlessness and chaos. Even the armed forces, in advanced countries, submit to the decisions of unarmed civilians as a matter of course, recognizing that the will of the majority as expressed through law and the constitution under which the state operates, is the very foundation on which society rests, providing security far more important than vindication in any specific issue.

Under our Constitution, with its system of checks and balances, the three great departments of Government, the legislative, the executive and the judiciary, are each bound by oath to support the basic law of the land and to avoid encroachment on the prerogatives of one another. Such restraint could not be enforced in the absence of ethics. The use of force by one of the divisions of our Government against the other would itself violate the constitutional provision of the separation of functions. The restraint is therefore a moral obligation, deriving from the oath of office, taken by every official of the Government to uphold the Constitution. So fully have the people recognized the significance of this ethical concept, that even the semblance of a violation of the spirit of the Constitution in this regard has been generally condemned throughout our history. It has become ingrained in our law and is really the genius of our institution.

But we are also sometimes painfully aware of the inability of law to solve problems of ethics. A ship is not a sea; and there are innumerable facets of our lives, with which the law cannot possibly deal. We learned the danger of trying to confuse what the people consider the realm of ethics with what they consider the realm of law in the bitter school of experience, during the era of Prohibition. An amendment to the Constitution of the United States, and the laws passed under it, were greatly resented by a large proportion of our people, perhaps the majority, as an invasion of private judgment by the nation. They felt that the amendment itself, and the laws passed under it, constituted an effort to use the machinery of the nation to compel obedience in an area of private life, where persuasion alone was indicated. After a number of years, we found that taking the issue of alcoholism out of the area of ethics and placing it in the area of government—instead of curbing the use of alcohol (which the effort did not succeed in doing), led otherwise law-abiding citizens to violate the law. The morals of the community were also being undermined in other areas than alcoholism itself. There arose a system of underworld organizations, leading to the spread of crime, with dire effects felt even to this day. Respect for law was undermined because law had tried to deal with a problem which in the modern world is considered one of ethics; and being undermined in part, tended to be undermined as a whole.

Not everything which is wrong can be outlawed, although everything which is outlawed, is, in our Western conception, wrong. For many years, legislatures and courts have endeavored to define for corporate and government officials what constitutes a conflict between their public responsibilities and their private interests. None has yet been able to state in legal terms rules that will at the same time afford both freedom of dynamic action by the individual and protection of the public interest. Every law designed for such a purpose has presumed and I assume must necessarily presume that such laws cannot be effective unless there is law behind the law; i.e., an ethical concept on the part of all who accept public responsibilities.

In the complexities of civilized life, we cannot, even in time of war, undertake to guide each individual in his moral decisions. Indeed, we feel that we should not. One of the purposes of civilized society is to produce men capable of making righteous decisions and adhering to them. To compel obedience in all areas of life would be to reduce men to automata, incapable of making their own moral decisions and defeating the very purpose of civilization itself.

We need law to guide us in areas properly subject to it. We decide through legal procedures, legislative, executive and judicial, how we should conduct ourselves in the vast areas of life subject to the scrutiny and power of society. A father may decide how his inheritance is to be divided among his children, and the courts will generally enforce his will. But the courts cannot compel his children to love one another, or even to behave as though they did. If courts could compel love, there would never be divorce. If courts could compel friendship, there would hardly be any litigation. If courts could compel mercy, many of the evils of our life would cease to exist.

It is even more difficult for courts to deal with problems which are utterly private. There is no way in which the legislature can outlaw selfishness or greed, or avarice, or cowardice, except in a few particularly gross manifestations. Law may require all of us to be vaccinated against some diseases, especially when we are threatened by an epidemic; but in general, it has no way of controlling habits, even those inevitably leading to disease.

Therefore, society would come to grief without ethics, which is unenforceable in the courts, and cannot be made part of law. If there were no sense of love in families, if there were no sense of loyalty, if friendship meant nothing, if we all, or any large proportion of us were motivated only by avarice and greed, society would collapse almost as completely as though it lacked law. Not only does law in civilized society presuppose ethical commitment; it presupposes the existence of a broad area of human conduct controlled only by ethical norms and not subject to law at all.

There is thus a law beyond the law, as binding on those of us who cherish our institutions as the law itself, although there is no human power to enforce it. Our economy rests to a great extent on the mutual faith of seller and . . . [buyer], which implies far more than the courts can possibly enforce. We enter a store and are offered an article at a certain price. In primitive communities, it is not possible for the purchaser to know whether the price is fair or not. To assure himself of fair dealing, the consumer must resort to a long process of bargaining, even over trivial objects. In civilized communities, such bargaining is limited to purchases which are distinctive and of large concern, like that of a house. But if one buys a necktie, one simply assumes that the prices stated by the vendor are fair ones for the object, and one pays it.

In the law beyond the law, which calls upon us to be fair in business, where the law cannot command fairness; which bids us temper justice with mercy, where the law can only enforce justice; which demands our compassion for the unfortunate, although the law can only give him his legal due, each of us is necessarily his own chief justice. In fact, he is the whole Supreme Court, from which there lies no appeal. The individual citizen may engage in practices which, on the advice of counsel, he believes strictly within the letter of the law, but which he also knows from his own conscience are outside the bounds of propriety and the right. Thus, when he engages in such practices, he does so not at his own peril—as when he violates the law—but at peril to the structure of civilization, involving greater stakes than any possible peril to himself.

This law beyond the law, as distinct from law, is the creation of civilization and is indispensable to it. Unknown to primitive societies, except to the extent that it is identified with the law itself, it has been transmitted from generation to generation in the family, in the school, in the great religious traditions and philosophies of the world.

The existence of this law beyond the law places heavy responsibilities on the individual. It is he who has to apply it in difficult and perplexing situations. This necessity requires him to be trained in the discernment of right from wrong and in the will to accept the right, without the slightest duress. His problem is the more complicated because the issues presented by life are rarely simple. The individual usually has no difficulty in discerning absolute wrong from absolute right, just as the Supreme Court would never be divided in its opinions if in a particular case only one constitutional principle were involved. It divides very frequently, because in actual cases, several constitutional principles are involved, and their implications, so far as these cases are concerned, are by no means the same. Similarly, the individual, confronted with life's problems, has to evaluate the relevance of one value or precept against another, insofar as both concern the immediate situation. No wonder that he is frequently perplexed; and wishes he could free himself from the obligation to follow the law beyond the law.

This ability properly to appraise different values in their relevance to specific issues, we call character. A person able to discern the right in the midst of great confusion and to pursue it, is a person of character. A person may be learned or ignorant; he may be old or young, rich or poor, well or sick; whatever his condition, he has to act; and his actions have their effect on himself and generally also on his fellow men. The man of character, sensitive to the meaning of what he is doing, will know how to discover the ethical path in the maze of possible behavior.

The importance attaching to educating men of character has been beautifully dramatized by the foremost of our poets in a series of plays which have become immortal. In his great tragedies, which after the lapse of three centuries still command our interest and admiration, Shakespeare with great compassion for the sad lot of man, illustrated how failure of character can lead to personal ruin and widespread catastrophe.

Brutus, as his adversary testified, was an honorable man. But as Shakespeare saw him, he had what Napoleon, himself no paragon of virtue, but in some respects a wise man, recognized as the most fatal defect of all—the inability to know his own limitations. Without imagination, he identified the Rome of his day with that of his famous ancestor who had defied the early kings of Rome, and Caesar with those kings. The great changes which had occurred since those early days in the responsibilities of Rome and her power apparently seemed to him negligible. He believed that by emulating his distinguished ancestor, he could perform for his own time the service which the earlier Brutus had performed for his community. But it was not so. A new world had developed; and if Caesar was wrong in trying to establish a dictatorship, Brutus was likewise morally obtuse in trying to preserve an outworn oligarchy calling itself a republic. The moral problems of Rome in his time arose from her world power; and had to be resolved not by return to the past, but by imaginative planning for the future. Of this Brutus was incapable. Error led to error; his agreement to murder Caesar led to a revulsion of conscience in which he spared Antony whom he allowed to speak at Caesar's funeral, and who inflamed the people against Brutus and the conspirators. War ensued; and Brutus had no alternative but to die at his own hands.

Hamlet represents a totally different type of person, but with equally astonishing defects of character, despite his nobility and attractiveness. Hamlet finds it almost impossible to resolve his moral dilemmas. Seeking guidance in sheer intellectual brilliance, he finds the problems presented by life almost incapable of solution. In his despair, he turns from intellect to impulse, murdering the innocent Polonius and driving his beloved Ophelia to insanity. When he ultimately decides that he must slay his uncle, he slays a whole series of other people, including himself, with him.

Macbeth is a loyal and brave warrior, whom, however, the apparition of witches is able to transform together with his wife, into rebels and regicides. His loyalty and devotion to his king is a ritual, unable to withstand the onslaught of the passion for power. One murder leads to others; rebellion leads to tyranny, and ultimately, Macbeth, who might have ended his life honorably, dies disgraced and heartbroken.

King Lear, perhaps the most tragic figure of all, wants to be loved and wants to be sure that he is loved. He wishes to bequeath his kingdom not according to the love he feels, but according to the love he persuades himself he receives. And in the quest for certainty of being loved—a quest necessarily vain—he disinherits the daughter who loves him most.

Although these characters differ markedly from one another, they have several traits in common, leading to their disasters. All of them share a certain naïveté in the affairs of life. None of them is really moved by compassion for individual human suffering and weakness. Three are moved to commit murder, and the fourth to the banishment of his youngest child. Shakespeare seems to be telling us that wisdom and compassion are indispensable ingredients of character and are basic to any true ethics. Compassion may not be adequate. To pity a child in such a way as not to wake him in time for school, is to hurt, not to help him. To indulge a weak person in his weakness, is to do him a disservice. There is need for compassion beyond compassion, as there is need for law beyond law. But we cannot dispense with sheer compassion if we desire to achieve right decisions.

The four tragic Shakespearean characters have another fatal quality in common. They all reach their disastrous decisions without consultation.

Shakespeare seems to be telling us that none of us is so perfect as to be able to rely solely on his individual judgment in moral issues, especially those which involve his deepest emotions. Compassion would have saved each of these characters from the harsh action he took; but doubtless so would consultation with people of high integrity, not personally involved in the problems.

The need for consultation is a recognized principle of legal procedure.

The Court over which I have the honor to preside would be a different court not only in wisdom, but also in character, if it consisted of only one person. Even in the law, where the issues are often less complicated than in our daily lives, each of us, participating in final authority, needs the frank and independent criticism of his peers. In our Court, any member may be outvoted, but no one is outvoted until after consultation and reflection upon the competing values involved in the problem to be solved. Likewise, in the areas in which each of us is his own court, so to speak, in the law beyond the law, one must be prepared to be outvoted after taking counsel with his better instincts and to accept graciously the minority status that follows.

We all know the importance of consulting a physician about our physical health. Is our moral health any less important? In one area of life, such moral counseling has been introduced with very significant results—namely that of marriage. The profession of the marriage counselor has achieved recognition and even distinction, and is doubtless responsible for the preservation of many families, which might otherwise have been broken.

But the business executive, the labor leader, the academician, the politician—needs counsel as to what is right no less than the husband and the wife. Our chairman, Judge Rifkind, is quoted as remarking that frequently when new business ventures are undertaken, all kinds of experts are present—except for one expert—the expert in ethics, who can suggest whether the whole plan as conceived was socially useful, was right, was appropriate under the circumstances.

It would require quite a revolution in our way of thinking for each industry to invite an expert in ethics to sit on its board and to participate in its deliberations; for each trade union to have such an expert advise it with regard to its responsibilities to the general community, as well as to its own members, and to advise its officers regarding their responsibility for the men under their guidance. Our college campuses might look very different if such problems as the promotion of faculty members, and the enlargement and functioning of the school itself were subject to deliberation on moral grounds. And our political campaigns, our nominations and elections might well be different, if political parties included experts in ethics among those deciding policies.

Is it fantastic to suggest that there is an urgent need in our troubled times for the development of the profession of the counselor in ethics, having the same relation to interpersonal conduct, beyond the law, that the lawyer has to conduct that is subject to the review in the courts? The developments of this century indicate that this need is no fantasy at all. Until this century, the world had never heard of marriage counselors or of psychoanalysts. Yet the value of each calling had been demonstrated. The search for ethics has been pursued since ancient times. Is it not obvious that all of us need ethics counselors?

Such counselors in ethics might well include the ministers of all faiths, if they were trained to serve in the capacity required of them by a changing world. Knowledge of the great traditions of ethics would certainly help an ethics counselor, no less than knowledge of legal precedent helps a lawyer, trying a case which is really without precise precedent. But in the contemporary world, ethics counselors might have to include other people than ministers, as well. I can conceive also of lay scholars who, having mastered the ethical thought of the ages and spent much time in the study of the modern world and its problem, could helpfully suggest courses of action and alternatives which might prove helpful to the modern businessman, politician, academic executive and other professionals who wish to discern the right. I can conceive of a school dedicated to the purpose of training such professionals, becoming the center of research in the field of moral standards, trying to resuscitate the glories of Aristotle, of Maimonides, of St. Thomas Aquinas and of Spinoza; and yet different from their ways of research in its concern with concrete problems of conduct, and training people to help themselves and to help others solve concrete issues of personal behavior. The education of both ministers of religion and of lay specialists, qualified to help the confused find himself in the maze of ethical problems is, in my opinion, one of the urgent needs of Western democracy, as it attempts to preserve its tradition of freedom in competition with rival systems of life, where once more, as in primitive life, all right conduct is dictated by law.

The businessman, the labor leader, the politician or the college executive may fear that with such an ethics counselor at his elbow, he might be discouraged from undertakings he has much at heart. But what in fact is the alternative to such discouragement of what is contrary to the public good, or the long-range good of mankind, or to simple compassion for the individual? Is it to proceed headlong as we are proceeding now, deifying success as the sole goal in life, and constantly putting greater emphasis on quantity rather than on quality in what we achieve? And if we proceed in this manner, is it not obvious that within a reasonable time—not too long—the whole world, emulating us Americans, even if it does not love us, will adopt the very standards which we have adopted? And when that happens, will it not turn out that we, like Brutus, Hamlet, Macbeth and King Lear, have brought on ourselves quite avoidable disaster?

It happens that at this climax of history, our country stands at the apex of world power, of world resources, of world wealth and of world influence. This is a great privilege, but it is a privilege carrying with it enormous responsibility. The responsibility which is ours is to stimulate mankind to conduct its affairs with wisdom, with conscientiousness, with a view to the future, with an understanding of the public need, with a view to the long-range perspectives of history, and above all, with great compassion for the individual.

The situation would be hopeless indeed if every village did not have its houses of worship, guided by ministers of the various faiths. These ministers are kept busy in our communities with various functions, all of them useful. They minister to the sick and the dying; they help the needy; they move us to recognize the greatness of our Creator and urge us to find a way to righteousness.

They are overburdened men. And yet the times require these dedicated servants of God to take on even another burden and willingly to share with others, not necessarily ordained, the task of analyzing the problems of the individual in the modern world. The seminaries in which ministers are trained need to prepare them for this service to the individual in the community, and they need to find a way to win the faith of the community leaders in industry and the professions in the guidance which they have to offer.

I believe that the Herbert II. Lehman Institute of Ethics, established at your seminary, and named for one of the truly eminent figures of our country and our time, can serve as a pilot project, in which to train such ethics counselors for men of your own faith, and through their example to stimulate the development of similar centers in other traditions. I do not regard the word of Scripture as a dead letter, addressed only to the generations who heard it from the mouths of the Prophets. I regard the Scriptures as a living tradition, as applicable in our time as in any other. But in a changing world, this word needs new interpreters, adventuresome spirits, able to make it effective in our lives.

If this task of making moral decisions a guide in our lives can be accomplished in our generation, we will have taken a giant step toward bringing ourselves closer to the idea to which men have been striving since the origin of the species. We will also, I believe, be doing much to prevent the moral decay of our community, a decay similar to that which has proven fatal to all earlier great empires and civilizations.

Wisdom and compassion are the indispensable ingredients of moral decision. We are all born compassionate, although as we grow older, we sometimes permit what we believe is practical to blind us to our innate mercy. Wisdom has to be acquired. It may be acquired in the family, in the school, in the church and synagogue, and in other institutions which civilization has created for that purpose. But there comes a time when the wisest of men finds himself confused, because as it is difficult for a client to serve as his own attorney, for a patient to be his own physician, so it is sometimes difficult for even the wisest and most learned of men to be his own counselor in ethics. The recognition that this role properly belongs to ministers of religion and is one of their gravest responsibilities, and that to carry out this responsibility in a changing world with innumerable problems, they may have themselves to seek guidance from experts in fields other than their own, may turn out to be indispensable to our civilization.

Our Constitution has guided our country for almost two centuries in a manner which might have surprised even its framers. It certainly has surprised many critical observers. A study of this Constitution reveals that it is permeated by the two qualities I have mentioned—wisdom and compassion. Wisdom and compassion also characterized the foremost of our statesmen, Abraham Lincoln, who has proven to be such an inspiration the world over.

In these examples, taken from the history of our nation, we can find a guide to help each of us in his individual decision. We need compassion; we need wisdom. In perplexity, when temptation turns us away from either or both, we need reliance on a guide who will remind us of their relevance to our lives, of their importance to ourselves as individuals, and because of our unique role in the history of our time, to the world which is emerging about us.

EDUCATIONAL PROBLEMS OF SEGREGATION AND DESEGREGATION OF PUBLIC SCHOOLS [3]

John H. Fischer [4]

On May 17, 1954, the Supreme Court unanimously declared racial segregation in the public schools unconstitutional. The decision ushered in a civil rights revolution which has unquestionably brought significant gains to a large part of our population. Moreover, it has given strength to the nation through legal affirmation of a basic right long denied to many citizens of Negro descent. Carrying out the decision has, however, not been easy everywhere; some of the necessary social and political adjustments have resulted in pain and bitterness, not to mention violence.

Speaking on May 3, 1962, at a conference convened in Washington, D.C., by the United States Commission on Civil Rights, Dr. John H. Fischer presented a succinct, provocative statement on the "purely educational dimensions" of desegregation and integration. Before becoming dean in 1959 and president in 1962 of Teachers College, Columbia University, Dr. Fischer was superintendent of public instruction in Baltimore. The prompt desegregation of the Baltimore school system took place under his administration. Besides Dr. Fischer, the panel session of May 3 was composed of Dr. Houston Jackson, assistant superintendent of the Baltimore public schools, and Dr. J. B. White, dean of the College of Education, University of Florida. About one hundred educators and community leaders attended the meeting.

Two theses stand out boldly in Dr. Fischer's speech: (1) "To achieve equality of opportunity within the whole of our culture, it may be necessary to offer those who are handicapped by their history or their current situation not merely equal, but compensatory educational opportunity." (2) "In organizing education many considerations are important, many characteristics are relevant, but racial differences in themselves are not. In the administration of schools . . . the manipulation of pupils on purely racial grounds is irrelevant and improper."

In the subsequent question-and-answer session, Dr. Fischer's point of view came in for extensive inquiry. Because they are pertinent to

---

[3] Text furnished by Dr. Fischer, with permission for this reprint. A full report, containing all the speeches and discussions of the Fourth Annual Education Conference on Problems of Segregation and Desegregation of Public Schools, was issued by the United States Commission on Civil Rights in 1962. I am indebted to Mr. Berl I. Bernhard, staff director of the commission, for supplying a copy.

[4] For biographical note, see Appendix.

his thesis and may possibly serve as springboards for discussion by students, selected excerpts from his replies follow:

> I have often said that the behavior of the teacher who says, "I don't want to teach in a difficult school," might be likened to a social worker who said, "I don't want to work with people who have family problems," or a psychiatrist who said, "I don't want to deal with people who are emotionally ill because I find it unpleasant."

> What we see is teachers declining to work with people who most need to learn and be educated.

> [With regard to] integrating student bodies, I would agree wholeheartedly that integrated student bodies are desirable and that they should be encouraged in every possible way, but I don't think that any child should be brought into any school as an exhibit for the edification of another child. This I also find offensive. It's using people as means rather than treating them as the supreme ends. I think that opportunities for integration ought to be provided through policy action and through administrative action, but I do not think that any governmental agency, any school board, or any school administrator ought to establish racial quotas or ratios.

> I would, within a given school district, in the sense of an area under a given board, if I had my way, completely abolish attendance districts and give any person who lived within the jurisdiction of that board the opportunity to enroll his child in any school within that total community.

> I don't know that it makes too much difference whether you record on a child's record card what his race is. I have never been able to get excited about that issue. I don't think it's wrong to record a child's race. I think it's wrong to discriminate against a child because of his race, but simply to acknowledge in writing that he is of Caucasian descent or of Negro descent or of Oriental background—this, in itself, is certainly not reprehensible practice. On the other hand, I don't care particularly whether it's done or not, so long as a teacher or others responsible for the child pay some intelligent attention to the child's needs and make an effort to find out as much about his background as is necessary to teach him well.

To say that the problems of race relations in the United States are complex hardly helps to clarify our situation, but unless the complexity of this matter is seen and taken constantly into account, no single step is likely to be very useful. The problems of American education are no less complex. In a nation as diversified as ours, universal education can never be simple, and it is universal education, with emphasis on both adjective and noun, that we must now achieve. As the issues of race relations permeate almost every aspect of our life, so events in our schools are interlaced with virtually everything we do or hope to do. The difficulties of operating schools which can cope successfully and, as they must, simultaneously with both racial and educational issues are therefore among the most puzzling of all the problems facing the American people.

The other side of the coin, however, is that the benefits that can flow from the solution of these two problems will be of a magnitude comparable to the difficulties themselves.

Virtually all the purposes for which our schools are maintained may be grouped under two major classifications. First, the school is expected to give every student the opportunity and the means to develop to the full whatever individual potentiality he may have. One purpose of the school, to say it more briefly, is to help each student make the most of himself.

The second purpose is related to the first but not entirely congruent with it. This is to induct the young person systematically into the culture and society to which he is an heir and in which he should be a partner. The school's success in respect to this purpose must be gauged not only by the competence of its graduates but by the quality of their sense of moral responsibility.

By viewing what we do with any child, of any race, against these considerations, one personal, the other racial, we should be able to reach reasonably sound conclusions about the effectiveness of our schools and the extent to which their performance approaches the ideals we project in our statements of philosophy.

Limitations of time make it impossible to include in this paper more than passing reference to the fact that the educational problems of desegregation and integration have important political, legal, and social aspects. I shall concentrate upon the more purely educational dimensions of the matter, which is to say its cultural and psychological aspects.

The temptation is always strong to say that the Negro child should be seen merely as any other child, respected as an individual, and provided with an educational program that will best meet his particular combination of needs. Of course the Negro child, like every other child, is entitled to be treated as an individual. Such treatment is the only sound basis for projecting his or any other child's education, but the easy generalization does not always come to grips with the whole truth.

The American Negro youngster happens to be a member of a large and distinctive group that for a very long time has been the object of special political, legal, and social action. This, I remind you, is not a question of what should be true, or might have been, but an undeniable and inescapable fact. To act as though any child is suddenly separable from his history is indefensible. In terms of educational planning, it is also irresponsible.

Every Negro child is the victim of the history of his race in this country. On the day he enters kindergarten, he carries a burden no white child can ever know, no matter what other handicaps or disabilities he may suffer. We are dealing here with no ordinary question of intercultural understanding, although admittedly cultural difference is a part of the difficulty. Nor are we concerned with only the usual range of psychoeducational problems, for the psychological situation of the Negro child is affected by quite special social considerations.

I recognize the hazard in speaking of "the Negro child." It is equally unsatisfactory to speak of "the white child" or "the Puerto Rican child" or "the Spanish American child" as though any child could be encompassed in a stereotype. Whatever a child's ethnic or racial background, he may be bright or slow, attractive or unpleasant; his parents may be rich or poor, well educated or illiterate, responsible or shiftless. Every racial group distributes itself in some fashion over the whole social and economic scale. But when all the variability is conceded, it cannot be denied that every American Negro child must expect to encounter certain problems which none of our other children face in quite the same way.

Many of the recent efforts to integrate Negro pupils into the mainstream of American public education have been built on the assumption that the problems are essentially administrative, legal, or political. As a consequence, we have seen drives for what is called "open enrollment" and other schemes to bring about, usually through directive action, a desired combination of races in particular classrooms or schools. Having worked in school administration for some twenty-seven years, I claim some knowledge of at least its limitations. Although, as you might suspect, I hold that administrative procedure and actions can be useful in education, I grow steadily more certain that no major problem of education—by which I mean really effective teaching and learning—has ever been solved solely, or even primarily, by legal or administrative action. To be sure, such action often lays the necessary groundwork and provides the setting in which good teachers may carry on their work, but the critical point in any educational system is found ultimately in the relation between the teacher and the pupil.

What, then, can be done to produce the sort of pupil-teacher relationship that will contribute most to the tasks we are thinking of today?

For one thing, we must continue to recognize the element of cultural difference. As the Educational Policies Commission pointed out in a recent statement, a principal part of the difficulty of what the commission calls the "disadvantaged American" is the fact that a substantial minority of Americans have grown up in cultures which are not compatible with much of modern life. This minority consists by no means only of Negroes, nor are all Negroes culturally disadvantaged. But vast numbers of them are, as a direct consequence of legal and social segregation.

The situation is not new. The mountain whites and rural Negroes, among others, have lived in cultural isolation for a long time. Now, however, the negative influence of poor economic conditions in their former homes combined with the positive illusory attraction of the city have caused a vast and growing migration. The congregation of tens of thousands of these people in places for which their customary living patterns are ill-adapted tragically dramatizes their cultural dislocation.

Many of the Negro children who now come to school are the victims of their parents' lack of knowledge and of schooling. The parents in turn are the victims of a situation over which they have had little or no control themselves. Parents and children alike elicit sympathy and attract charity, but praiseworthy as these responses may be, they form no adequate approach to the education of the disadvantaged urban child. The response of the community and the school must be based also on objective knowledge and mature understanding of the underlying difficulty and an inventive turn of mind among teachers and administrators. Teaching reading, for example, to a first grade child who has never seen an adult read anything requires an approach quite different from one appropriate to a child in whose home books are as normal as food.

Similarly, a child who has never known sustained conversation with his parents must actually learn the skills of continuing discussion before he can learn much else in school.

Nor is it enough to say that the school should accept the child where it finds him and raise him as high and as fast as it can toward an adequate level of cultural attainment. To be sure, this is one of the school's functions; no teacher ever succeeds unless he first establishes rapport and communication with the pupil at the pupil's level. But the school's procedure and its success will necessarily differ between the child whose home background daily complements what the school does, and the one who is caught, so to speak, in a cultural downdraft the moment he steps outside the school.

In dealing with a population which is racially and culturally integrated, the school must begin by encouraging teachers to understand the special factors in the backgrounds of all their children, to take these differences imaginatively into account, and to build curricula and teaching techniques that reflect not only idealism but realism as well.

In addition to the cultural aspect, intellectual considerations are involved in meeting the problems of racial integration. A good school is responsibly concerned with all of the aspects of a child's development, but the central purpose that must run through all sound education is the development of intellectual strength. Unless the school is able to help every child to use his mind effectively, none of the other purposes of education can be satisfactorily achieved. We customarily cite physical health as a fundamental goal of education, but unless the child learns to apply his own intelligence to the problem of remaining healthy, he is not likely to do much either for his own well-being or for the public health of his community. The young person who does not become critically thoughtful about moral values, who behaves well only when someone is watching him or forcing him to conform, cannot be trusted to manage his own morality. But the school's success in pursuing this central purpose of education is subject, like so many of its other efforts, to what happens to the pupil outside the school.

In respect to the development of intellectual competence, many Negro children face special problems that should be better understood than they often are. Obviously many Americans of Negro ancestry have attained distinction in fields requiring intellectual eminence and millions of others daily apply their minds with excellent results in more humble ways. Yet the fact remains that during years of oppression, first under slavery and later under more subtle forms of discrimination, the opportunities for large numbers of Negroes to apply their own rational powers with initiative and freedom to important problems have been far more limited than the opportunities available to other racial groups. Many Negro children, therefore, carry the disabling scars of the culture in which they were nurtured, a culture which encouraged the use of muscles and not only discouraged but often penalized those who sought to use their minds creatively. The school must take all of this into account and build programs and provide opportunities which not only reflect these facts but move aggressively to compensate for them.

Every educational problem has its emotional side, and the special problems of educating Negro children in desegregated schools have theirs. Not being a psychologist, I do not intend to examine this complex question at any length. But there can be little doubt that the education of many Negro children is adversely affected by emotional considerations. The fact that it is often difficult to distinguish among the cultural, the intellectual, and the emotional aspects of education is one reason why teaching any child is so complex.

One of the most serious of the details is the problem of motivation. The Horatio Alger story is a well-established part of our folklore, but few Americans would argue that the typical Alger hero would have made it had his skin been of a darker shade. The sense of frustration which any minority child may experience is heightened in the case of the Negro child, who discovers all too early that his minority has both a special history in the United States and quite unique problems. As a consequence, his attitude toward himself and toward his racial group complicates the effort to help him secure an adequate education. In some cases, he may rationalize his failures by attributing them to limitations which do not, in fact, exist for him. In others, he may develop an understandable aggressiveness which will neither compensate for external difficulties nor correct his own shortcomings. The wise and well-informed teacher is aware of these emotional complications and undertakes to deal with them in positive ways.

In the face of these facts, and in the light of our democratic values, what guidelines for policy and practice in the conduct of American public schools are implied?

In the first place, it is essential to emphasize on every possible occasion and in everything we do in schools that the rights of students, the assessment of their needs, and the release of their potentialities must be approached on an individual basis. What I have said about the identification of students as members of groups is important only insofar as it helps the teacher to understand a particular student. My point, you may remember, is that the individual cannot be understood unless he is seen against the history from which he has come and in terms of the situation in which he currently lives. But his education is peculiarly his own. The opportunities afforded any child may not properly be limited because he happens to be a member of one or another racial group. In this connection, again, we face the hazard of stereotyped treatment, a hazard which at all costs must be avoided.

This implication for policy and practice cuts more than one way, however, for just as certainly as no person should be subjected to discriminatory treatment which depresses him because of his race, so it follows that none should be given preferential treatment simply because his complexion or his ancestry is different from another's. A practical application of this principle may arise if a school organizes classes according to the academic ability of students. If, after the most reliable estimates of ability the school can make, it should develop that one classroom contains pupils largely of one racial group while a second classroom is composed mostly of another, the school should not be criticized for the result. If, on the other hand, the school authorities have used an ostensibly educational device simply to justify some predetermined racial arrangement, the action is totally indefensible. It should be attacked not only as a violation of the constitutional rights of children but as a flagrant instance of professional malpractice.

A second guideline for the development of policy and practice centers about the concept of equality of opportunity. "Equality of opportunity," as we customarily use the phrase, means much more than a schoolroom desk for every child. It connotes, rather, a condition in which every American may rightfully expect to find himself in fair competition with every other American. This condition is achieved and maintained by the operation of a host of agencies and forces, some political, some social, others economic or cultural. The public school has never been the only agency concerned with producing equality of opportunity, but its role is fundamental to the total effort.

In the cases of some Americans, and in that of the Negro American most dramatically, our traditional system has failed for a long time and in countless ways to provide that equality of opportunity that should be the condition of all our people. Recent improvements have helped correct the imbalance, but much more correction is required. Especially is this true of children whose parents and grandparents were deliberately, systematically and by law denied what is now clearly recognized as fully equal treatment.

Is it not a reasonable contention—and a just one—that to compensate for past injustice, we should offer these children educational services beyond the level of what might be called standard equality?

Could it be that to achieve total equality of opportunity in America we may have to modify currently accepted ideas about equality of opportunity in education itself? Is it conceivable that some of our children are entitled to more and better educational opportunities than most of the others? In fact, of course, the question has already been answered. Thousands of mentally and physically handicapped children, regardless of race, regularly receive teaching service, physical facilities, and supporting services more extensive and more costly than those furnished children who are considered physically or mentally normal. In the cases of many Negro children—and the generalization would apply also to certain other minority groups—we may need to substitute for our traditional concept of equal opportunity a new concept of compensatory opportunity.

Such compensatory opportunity might take the form of lower student-teacher ratios in certain schools, or additional guidance services, or better physical facilities. The idea might mean more scholarships for higher education, or, in some cases, custodial and boarding care for children whose welfare required their removal from a crippling environment.

I doubt that anyone is in a position now to say precisely what the concept of compensatory educational opportunity would mean in every case, but my purpose here is not so much to answer the question as to raise it for discussion. The concept of compensatory opportunity should certainly not be restricted to any one group and, as I have suggested, it has already been applied to other types of disability. But, to the degree that a child's race or cultural background handicap him, and especially where they are attributable, at least in part, to earlier governmental action, they should be taken into account in adjusting his educational program.

A third guide to educational policy and practice seems relevant to this discussion. If we are to keep the focus of our educational effort on the welfare of the individual child, we shall do well to avoid what is sometimes called social engineering. The very term is inconsistent with the purposes and values of democracy. Even the most desirable end does not justify manipulating people to create a structure pleasing to some master planner. To put it precisely, I am disturbed about the growing pressure to locate schools, draw district lines, and organize curricula in order to achieve a predetermined racial pattern of enrollment. By no means am I opposing the desirability of having in the same school children of different racial backgrounds. Quite the contrary! But decisions about school organization based entirely or primarily on racial criteria seem to me to violate the principle of nondiscrimination. All school districting arrangements should provide a maximum of free choice for all children, subject only to common sense protection against unnecessary overcrowding. Indeed, if I had my way, I should have no school attendance districts at all. In a well-conducted school system every school should be so good that those who live near it would never think of going elsewhere except for some extraordinary reason. In the case of secondary schools, or others where specialized curricula might be a factor, the importance of the neighborhood location would, of course, be somewhat less significant. But here again the greatest possible freedom of choice should be allowed all pupils, so long as they are qualified for the programs involved.

The concept of freedom of choice should be interpreted, however, only to allow positive choice and never to permit any group to restrict the opportunities of another. The basic principle is that all public schools of a community belong to all the people of the community, that none is the exclusive preserve of a single racial group.

The most offensive aspect of the engineered approach is the assumption that any group can be improved if members of another race are introduced into it. If all the races of mankind are equally to be valued and respected, a group composed of thirty members of race A cannot be improved merely by substituting a few members of race B. If, on the other hand, the group is to be improved with regard, let us say, to mathematical performance, the introduction of a couple of mathematical wizards will obviously raise the average. A musical group short of tenors can surely be improved by recruiting three good tenors, but the point of origin of their grandfathers or the color of their hair are scarcely relevant criteria. We cannot have it both ways: we cannot say that race per se makes no difference and then argue that important decisions should be based on this inconsequential factor.

To summarize then, briefly what I have tried to say about the educational problems of desegregating schools:

1. The focus of sound teaching is always on the individual, for education is an intensely personal matter, having its principal effect always within the person.

2. If we are to achieve good education, we must respect the individuality of each student, relating his instruction to his background, his needs, his possibilities.

3. To achieve equality of opportunity within the whole of our culture, it may be necessary to offer those who are handicapped by their history or their current situation not merely equal, but compensatory educational opportunity.

4. In organizing education many considerations are important, many characteristics are relevant, but racial differences in themselves are not. In the administration of schools, therefore, the manipulation of pupils on purely racial grounds is irrelevant and improper.

A FLAVOR FOR OUR DAILY BREAD [5]

SAMUEL B. GOULD [6]

Dr. Samuel B. Gould is one of a sizable company of educators who in recent years have turned their talents and administrative skills to television. Former head of the communication arts department at Boston University and later president of Antioch College (1954-1959) and chancellor of the University of California at Santa Barbara (1959-1962), Dr. Gould is now president of the Educational Broadcasting Corporation in New York. The corporation he heads operates Channel 13, which serves the metropolitan areas of New York City and near-by New Jersey and Connecticut. It is an independent station chartered by the New York State Board of Regents, and is supported largely by contributions from individuals, business and industry, and foundation grants. Since its opening in late 1962, the station has built an enviable record of educational and public service.

Dr. Gould considers television a potentially powerful "educative force in society"; for those of similar conviction he foresees exciting opportunities "to be of service, to be creative, and to work in behalf of those values that make for a better life." He touches briefly upon this theme in an inspirational address delivered on November 7, 1962, before the students and faculty of Hunter College of the City University of New York. The speech received a warmly enthusiastic response.

Much has been written about youth's apolitical outlook, its preoccupation with guaranteed security and fringe benefits in preference to the challenges of adventure, and its seeming lack of commitment to anything beyond the satisfactions of the present moment. In his address, Dr. Gould assesses certain motivations which determine the directions in which modern college students move. And he doubts the validity of the usual characterizations of youth. In fact, he believes that the "most realistic attribute of today's American college student is his zeal to share somehow in the making of a better world."

I can't begin to tell you what a pleasure it is for me to be here with you today. As a former college and university head, when I am asked to meet with students I react like the proverbial old fire horse to the alarm. In the few short months that have

---

[5] Text furnished by Dr. Gould, with permission for this reprint.

[6] For biographical note, see Appendix.

represented such a considerable change in my life, what I find I miss most is the students, those unpredictable, fantastic, irrepressible students who used to drive me to distraction at one moment and charm me into willing submission the next. My wife and I still think back nostalgically over the evening conversations with student groups on everything from free love to John Birchism, and the mountains of food that used to disappear like manna in the morning sun. Television is exciting but in a different and less personal way. To be close to youth is a rare privilege, and being with you today is in a sense like coming back home.

You will forgive me, I hope, if I am very unscholarly on this occasion and talk about something very simple. You can put away your notebooks and relax. Either you will remember something of what I say merely by listening and reacting, or it will not be worth bothering about. This is not a lecture but a conversation, and I wish it could be a many-sided one from the very start.

Everything I want to tell you is reflected in an incident that occurred to me several years ago, an incident that in and of itself has nothing to do with education and yet has everything to do with life. This is a true story.

A few summers ago I had occasion to spend some time in Colorado and one day chanced to stop at an Indian trading post. The post was operated by a descendant of the Blackfoot tribe, a man with the magnificent name of Charles Eagle Plume. His background, I discovered, was as magnificent as his name, for he was very well educated with an advanced degree in anthropology and a considerable amount of work behind him in the study of the history and habits of his people. His loyalty and devotion to the cause of the American Indian were quickly apparent as was his sense of bitterness over how they have been treated.

After some little conversation, Charles Eagle Plume took me upstairs in the post headquarters to show me some rare objects he had collected as part of his researches. One of these in particular he took out of its repository only after telling me the story behind it. It is this episode that I should like to share with you.

In 1851 a group of Indians lived at the mouth of the Sacramento River, a completely primitive tribe. Their homes were miserable huts built on marshy land, and the tribe was known as the Diggers. They had none of the arts we associate with other tribes, arts such as the gaily decorated baskets of the Cherokees or beautifully designed rugs of the Navajos. They merely existed.

One day during that year of 1851 a contingent of gold prospectors came to where these Indians lived and within the space of a few hours mercilessly wiped out the entire tribe, men, women and children alike. Practically every vestige of their existence was destroyed, but a few reminders of them survived and were eventually found.

At this point in his story, Charles Eagle Plume paused, his eyes still blazing with anger as he recalled the brutality of the gold miners. He took from a case behind him a tiny, closely woven basket no more than four inches in diameter and cradled it carefully in his hands.

Imagine if you will [he said] a native woman of this primitive tribe, a woman who had never had a single object of beauty in her whole life either to see or to possess. What she had been taught of basket weaving was only for utility, for the day-to-day needs of her household. Yet somewhere within her stirred an indefinable yearning, the awakening of a sense of awareness of beauty and loveliness, a craving to create something which would bring joy to her heart as she looked at it. And so, in an almost miraculous way, she wove this basket. When she had moments to herself she trapped quail and pulled out the tufts of black on their heads. Or she sat patiently, hour after hour, completely motionless, holding a flower in her hands and waiting for a hummingbird to come and feed. When it did, she closed her hands over it and plucked from its throat the tiny downy red feathers. Or again, she searched along the marshy shore for the tiniest and most perfect of shells. All these things she fashioned into her basket with no knowledge of design or craftsmanship, with nothing but this overwhelming urge to create.

And then Charles Eagle Plume uncupped his hands, and I saw the little basket. Around its rim was carefully placed a row of perfectly matched shells, the smallest I have ever seen. The black quail tufts were interspersed with these. And all through the tightly woven reeds of the basket were the throat feathers of the hummingbirds, forming a simple pattern of reddish cast, with a texture reminding one of the softness of thistledown. It was simple and primitive, but it was almost heart-rending, for one could not look at its artless grace without thinking of the poor girl whose yearnings had culminated in the creation of this single object, her only treasure.

Here was a life of drudgery, of hardship, and ultimately of tragedy. But it had within it the flavor of creativity that gave it a desire to know beauty, perhaps even a zest for living. This is the flavor that turns making a living into an exciting career, that makes of every activity a meaningful, moving, and sometimes even an uplifting experience.

You are not too far away from making some choices about the directions your life will take and the kind of career you will pursue. It may be that after you have chosen you will find reasons to change your mind more than once. These reasons in and of themselves are not so important except in terms of the motivations that occasion them. Perhaps you will allow me to spend a few moments discussing these motivations and then to tie some of them together with a specific example or two.

One of the motivations most often mentioned or at least thought about is that of security. The modern generation of youth has been accused again and again of being more security-minded than any other. It has been said that college graduates tend to look for positions with good starting salaries and a certain amount of guaranteed continuity, assuming their work is satisfactory. We are told that they ask more questions about fringe benefits and comfortable working conditions than they do about the challenge of the work. They shy away from precarious or impecunious occupations and are rather conservative in their views of how they should place themselves in society.

In spite of the number of times I have heard this characterization of modern youth, I am always inclined to be skeptical about it. In fact, I seem to sense quite a different feeling when I talk with young men and women, a yearning that relates itself to much higher and less selfish motivations. For example, I find an increasing tendency on their part to turn more and more toward a desire to be of service in the world. Even when I get letters from present-day college students commenting cynically about their disillusionment with the world as it is, with the blunderings of their elders, with the hypocrisies they see on every side—even then—I sense that as an undercurrent of this cynicism and bitterness is a tremendous eagerness to find some constructive way to help and to be a part of something worth while. Careers of teaching and research or of social and professional service appear to be more and more of interest to this college generation, and I interpret this motivation to be stimulated by youth's eagerness to associate themselves with intellectual life and the betterment of the world.

Perhaps I am being naïve and idealistic in this reaction, but I don't think so. I have been around college and university campuses too long to be completely fooled. No matter how he or she tries to hide behind a cloud of pseudosophistication or under a veneer of boredom, no matter how rebellious he or she may be about conventions or values or moral codes, the most realistic attribute of today's American college student is his zeal to share somehow in the making of a better world.

Coupled with this desire to be of service is the motivation toward creative satisfaction. A great part of individual unhappiness and emotional stress among modern adults stems from the frustrations that develop when one becomes convinced that his work has within it no creative spark and that he is, in truth, on a monotonous and unrewarding treadmill. This is not to say that there are no problems or frustrations when one is doing the work he loves and when he is sure of its many creative possibilities. But these problems and frustrations are all bearable so long as the promise of creative satisfaction exists. It is the capstone of the humanistic approach to life, and there is no substitute for it.

Suppose we consider just two examples, examples I choose deliberately because they come out of my personal experience. The first is a career in teaching, a profession rarely understood except by those who are part of it and have an almost fanatical devotion to it. Some years ago I tried to write my own definition of a teacher, and inadequate as it may be, let me repeat it to you because I believe it to be the truthful essence of this profession:

To me, a teacher is a person with a touch of immortality. . . . The desire to teach is a deep-seated one and permeates the hearts and souls of thousands upon thousands who have never given conscious thought to entering the profession. We all teach in one way or another, and in such activity we find unusual and almost mysterious satisfaction. The mother and father in daily contacts with their children are teaching constantly: teaching the baby to talk; teaching the young fry to swim, to fish, to read, to sing; teaching habits of living and thinking, sometimes by precept and sometimes by example. Children teach one another in their play; colleagues in business teach one another in their professional associations; physicians try whenever possible to devote a portion of their time to teaching medical students; concert artists are drawn to young people of talent; ministers are engaged in one of the noblest forms of teaching; and so we might go on and on. Why does this happen? Because we all sense, directly or indirectly, consciously or unconsciously, that to leave a vestige of oneself in the development of another is a touch of immortality. Through this we live far beyond our span of mortal years. Through this we find new and more impelling reasons for being, for populating the earth.

If you have ever seen the light of understanding shine in another's eyes where no light shone before, if you have ever guided the unsteady and unpracticed hand and watched it suddenly grow firm and purposeful, if you have ever watched a young mind begin to soar to new heights and have sensed that you are participating in this unfolding of the intellect, then you have felt within you the sense of being a humble instrument in the furtherance of mankind. Just as the doctor feels the heartbeat grow stronger under his ministrations and is overwhelmed by the goodness and the privilege vouchsafed to him in the performance of this service for another, so each person who teaches has an awareness of this same goodness and privilege. He knows that he lives in another being, and such knowledge fills him with ineffable love and gratitude. It counterbalances all the drudgery, the heartaches, and the sacrifices which are part of every worth-while profession. And most of the time, because he fears being called naïve or sentimental, he secretes this feeling deep within himslf and says nothing about it. . . . But the feeling persists, all the same.

Yes, a teacher is a person with a touch of immortality, and he should be most envied among men. His profession should be the most sought after, the most carefully prepared for, the most universally recognized. And believe me, as America grows in mental and cultural stature, it *will* be.

The second example has to do with educational television, an activity that is really just beginning to come into its own in America after ten years of effort. For the person who truly sees this medium of communication as an educative force in society, here is an opportunity to be of service, to be creative, and to work in behalf of those values that make for a better life.

Educational television, when it is properly interpreted and programed, deals with ideas and aesthetic appreciations. The ideas, if wisely chosen, relate to the heart of living. They impinge upon the philosophical, the social, the economic, the international consciousness of a people. Similarly, the aesthetic appreciations, since they come out of a new knowledge of and a closer familiarity with the great performing arts, broaden and deepen the spirit of man. Music, art, the dance, drama—every art form contributes to this all-important dimension and makes it as nourishing to the total life of the individual as food and drink.

The creative satisfactions that come from successful efforts to present this new and additional kind of television are illustrative of the flavor that can be added to one's daily work. Much of the preparatory work in programing may seem humdrum as well as arduous; the technical and staging difficulties may so absorb the mind that for a time the original idea becomes secondary to the mechanics, and the creative conception is submerged. But at the moment of successful presentation the creative impulse that motivated the program suddenly is clear again, and for those who have molded that impulse into a clear intellectual or aesthetic message, the reward is instantaneous and rich.

Many if not all careers can have within them this selfsame flavor, if we properly examine the validity of our reasons for entering them and the nature of the results we hope to achieve. Even the career of homemaking, so often scorned these days and so regularly misinterpreted, can be developed with a depth of creativity and understanding that will give new and badly needed strength to the American family in the face of rapidly eroding human values.

Whatever the career and whatever the task, it deserves what is best and finest in us. We must search constantly for the spark that makes dullness glow or envelops mediocre and half-hearted efforts with such a white-hot flame of effort that the result cannot help but be truly worthy. The spark is there, of that you may be sure. It remains for each of us to find it.

B. J. Chute, the writer, tells a wonderful story about a small child who watched a sculptor working on a slab of marble. Day after day, the child watched and the sculptor worked. And then, at last, there came a day when the child drew in his breath and looked at the sculptor in amazement and said, "But how did you know there was a lion in there?"

To know there is a lion in one's mind, and finally to produce it—that is success. That is the flavor for our daily bread, the closest we shall ever come to human happiness.

FRANCE-AMERICAN SOCIETY SPEECH [7]

Lauris Norstad [8]

For some fourteen years the North Atlantic Treaty Organization has represented both a hope and a promise of reasonable security for Western Europe and the free world. In recent years, however, doubts have arisen periodically as to the health of the organization. Back in March 1960, editor John Fischer of *Harper's Magazine* likened the plight of the Western alliance to that of Valencia about eight hundred years ago. When its bold leader, El Cid, died of old age, the Valencians propped the corpse on the back of his horse and ventured forth to battle. But the dead leader had indeed lost his awesomeness, the Moors soon discovered, and Valencia fell. Mr. Fischer asserted that NATO, like El Cid, is dead and can no longer wield the sword.

In recent months considerable disagreement has developed over the purpose of NATO. Following General de Gaulle's decision to keep Britain out of the Common Market and to look askance at President Kennedy's hope for an interdependent Atlantic community, both friends and foes of the French position called for a reassessment of our European commitments. Understandably, perhaps, many Europeans and particularly the French have fears of what they view as a monopoly of nuclear deterrence. They want independent nuclear capability or at least a greater share in the direction of a multilateral force. This touches upon the delicate issue of national sovereignties. According to Ronald Steel, writing in *Commentary* of December 1962, "all the declarations of interdependence are not going to breathe life into the alliance, so long as the United States continues to insist on a nuclear monopoly." Against this background, General de Gaulle projects his ambition, or more properly his vision, of a United Europe extending from the Atlantic to the Urals, with France as a central force.

In his short speech before the France-American Society in New York City on January 29, 1963, General Lauris Norstad, supreme commander of the military forces of NATO from 1956 through 1962, and now president of Owens-Corning Fiberglas International, reiterated his faith in "the full pattern of the Atlantic Community" with responsibilities collectively shared by the fifteen member countries. The youngest Air Force officer ever to become a four-star general, Norstad combines in his speak-

---

[7] Text furnished by George R. Medinnus, press relations manager, Owens-Corning Fiberglas Corporation, with permission for this reprint.

[8] For biographical note, see Appendix.

ing a full measure of ethical appeal and sensitive adaptation of subject matter, however delicate, to the particular audience. Students will find this talk essentially in low key. The topic is severely limited in scope; the treatment is artfully simple. But the handling of the theme is strikingly deft.

First of all, I would like to express my very great pleasure at being here this evening. Your society embodies—your presence here gives substance to—an idea, an ideal, that goes back to the very first days of the Republic—the friendship and close alliance of two great countries. This relationship through the centuries has brought much of value to France and the United States. In fact, neither of us would be quite the same today had not the other played its part in history. For without France in the eighteenth century the United States might never have emerged so surely fixed in its continental independence, and without the United States in the twentieth century, France might not now be so secure in its historic position in the heart of Europe.

My wife and I are home again after twelve years in Europe. I was about to say "of living abroad." But that rather genteel term, with its suggestion of a casual and comfortable expatriatism scarcely fits our circumstances. In Europe, I was not only an American officer with certain responsibilities for supporting United States' interests, but also an international officer charged with serving the interests of Europe. My work required me to measure matters connected with the defense of Europe through the European view as well as the one that was my birthright. I have come from that experience with a deep affection for Europe, with admiration for the ways that are unique to Europe and with a sense of marvel for those things of the spirit—the love of freedom and independence—that we and they have in common. I was made to feel at home in Europe, and I shall never forget that.

Under the particular circumstances of my service, I am bound by allegiance to all Europe. But in truth, there is a special relationship with the country in which I lived for almost twelve years. For one thing, France is the host of the alliance. SHAPE headquarters is at Rocquencourt, close to Paris; and the French presence infuses SHAPE's daily affairs. The French flag alone stands with the flag of NATO in fixed majesty at the entrance to the headquarters. The flags of the fourteen other countries rotate from day to day around them. Moreover, the stirring strains of the "Marseillaise" have through the years come to be used as the anthem of the alliance.

But in a much more personal way, France was our home. It was there we lived in a community whose life and activity we were privileged to share. All of you know France well and so will understand our feelings now. France and Paris have a chemistry all their own. I was reminded of this the other day when I came across a passage in a book of reminiscences by the Canadian writer Morley Callaghan. He is describing his first night in Paris when he and his wife, sitting at a sidewalk cafe, were strongly aware of that strange sense of homecoming even on first arrival, something we have all experienced. He writes:

Paris was around us and how could it be alien in our minds and hearts even if no Frenchman ever spoke to us? What it offered to us was what it had offered to men from other countries for hundreds of years; it was a lighted place where the imagination was free.

A lighted place! What a wonderful image. And indeed one of the richest experiences of my life, after arriving in Europe just as the postwar reconstruction was getting under way, was to see the darkness lift as in country after shattered country the lights of hope, of rekindled purpose, blazed up again.

Only a year or two ago, the transformation of Europe was being hailed as a miracle. I wonder. True, the capital provided by the Marshall Plan helped to set the process of recovery in motion. But, as is the case with all modern miracles, and certainly those of a political and economic nature, a fantastic amount of hard work also went into the job. We Americans helped greatly, but the Europeans also greatly helped themselves. In the Ruhr, in England's industrial midlands, in the war-broken cities of Belgium and the Netherlands, across France and Italy, ancient communities drew upon their skills and revived energies to rebuild what had been lost.

They did more, in fact. The Europe we contemplate now, in the high noon of its growth and self-assertiveness, is truly a *new* Europe. And nowhere are its rising strength and dynamism more evident than in France.

As a friend of France, I have been impressed by the multiplying signs of growth and progress—the new factories and buildings of all kinds, the roads, the power plants, but more even than these, the new drive and energy of the people. Americans have a particular affection for France; we want to see her prosper. And, being reasonable people, we do not begrudge her the right to say whatever she may feel needs saying with regard to the conduct of the alliance which binds the United States to her, and the two of us to the other nations of the alliance.

Yet, as we listen to what France appears to be saying, we would do well to keep in mind what the alliance expects of its members. For the conditions of the alliance impose upon all of us, on both sides of the Atlantic, a superior obligation; and in the beginning it was the resolution to meet this obligation, combined with the singular capacity of the United States to rearm Europe, while fostering its economic recovery, that made so many fine things possible.

The goals are set forth in the North Atlantic Treaty. Certainly the improved status of Europe is the best measure of our progress toward the achievement of the high aims established by our countries when, in these words, they reaffirmed

their faith in the purposes and principles of the Charter of the United Nations and their desire to live in peace with all peoples and all governments.

When they expressed their determination

to safeguard the freedom, common heritage and civilization of their peoples, founded on the principles of democracy, individual liberty and the rule of law [and] to promote stability and well-being in the North Atlantic area.

And when they

resolved to unite their efforts for collective defense and for the preservation of peace and security.

The current situation within the alliance should be seen in the perspective of these goals and the long climb toward them. In recent weeks the relationship of France to certain of its allies, and in fact, to the alliance as a whole has taken a worrisome turn. Let us not be so foolish as to minimize the seriousness of what is happening. It is only proper, as the European countries come into resources of their own, that they should wish a stronger voice in our common affairs. To meet these demands, the rules and relationships within the alliance are going to be reshaped somehow. The question is how, and whether the change is to be more in the way of a return to narrow national interests or toward an ever-broadening mutual endeavor.

We Americans, on our part, must show a willingness to consider the views, the special needs, of others. If we do this, we will be justified in expecting that our allies, who have grown so mightily over the past decade, will act in increasing awareness that with strength, with recognition, with authority, come a greater burden of responsibility, an increasing obligation to the world beyond national borders.

Some current problems are stated in terms of weapons, how they should be organized, how their use would be directed. Nuclear weapons, because of their vast power, have become a symbol of authority, of prestige, of sovereignty. It is understandable, therefore, that they should loom so large in the policy considerations of nations.

It is only reasonable that Europeans should give thought to all means of defense and, since the preservation of freedom is as dear to them as it is to us, they feel just as dependent as we do on the most modern types of equipment. Most of our allies are convinced that nuclear weapons, in some number, are necessary to their defense. They feel they need a guarantee that the weapons on which they must place such great dependence will continue to be available to them under all reasonable circumstances. Further, they feel that their responsibility to their own people as well as to the alliance requires that they have a voice, some substantial influence, in making the decisions which would govern the employment of this important means of defense. They are particularly interested in what is clearly the crux of this great problem—where will the authority reside and how will it be used?

Last week, here in New York, that great Frenchman, "Mr. Europe," Jean Monnet, emphasized this when he said, "You, in the United States, must realize that the claim of Europe to share common responsibility and authority for decisions on defense, including the nuclear weapons, is natural since any decision involves the very existence of the European peoples."

The responsibility "for collective defense and for the preservation of peace and security" in the vital European area, is, and should be, a collective one, a responsibility shared by *all* of the fifteen member countries. I believe that the NATO Council can organize itself to supervise and direct the development of the nuclear capability of the alliance, insuring that the interests of *all* fifteen countries are represented, that *all* views are considered. It can thus give real substance to the alliance as a political authority *in fact*.

I agree with Jean Monnet that our European allies have a natural, legitimate interest in sharing common responsibility and authority for decisions on important aspects of the common defense. If at the moment this is a problem, it is a problem that is the product of success. If it raises a serious question before the alliance, the answer to that question will be forthcoming. The very act of coming to grips with it should strengthen the moral fibers of the alliance.

As I suggested earlier, this is a time of change: truly we live on a watershed of history. Increasingly conscious of its growing strength, Europe is showing particular interest in development of new political alignments, in defining a new system of relationships. Until quite recently it appeared that the natural trends in Europe, as well as some direct and indirect influences from this side of the Atlantic, were directing the emphasis toward a "European" solution—toward the creation of a European "bloc" to balance the power, the strength, found in North America.

It is time to take a good long second look at this idea and, fortunately, the Europeans seem to be doing just that. It is recognized, of course, that there are certain specific functions which call for smaller regional groupings. Further, it is accepted that such smaller groupings may be essential intermediate steps toward a more complete and satisfactory pattern. However, it is encouraging to see the growing will to maintain the broader association of the fifteen countries which has been developed in NATO. There is an increasing desire to retain what has been tried and proved and what has added stature and dignity to all countries, large and small.

The Europeans will themselves define the future Europe and will establish its relationship with other countries or groups of countries in the West. That a thoughtful second look is now being taken adds to our faith that our partners will choose wisely and in the common interest. It is my own conviction, strongly held, that the pattern of the future must be the *full pattern* of the Atlantic Community. This, I believe, should be taken as the *ultimate objective*.

About a year ago, distinguished citizens of almost all nations in the Atlantic area met in Paris. They declared "that our survival as free men, and the possibility of progress for all men, demand the creation of a true Atlantic Community." This declaration is one we can support.

If we think that we in our time have a monopoly on difficulties, we have but to look back to see that in almost every age the troubles have been sufficient unto the day. But it may well be that no generation has faced such a complex and exacting responsibility as the one before us. The risk of disastrous war must be reduced, but we cannot live without liberty. That can never be placed in hazard.

In summing up, I would say that the problems now besetting the alliance are those which flow in good part from its own success. None of these problems are so vexing or so difficult that it could not be resolved by recourse to the willingness to understand which has already carried us so far together.

The late Henry Stimson, as far back as 1947, in a truly prophetic passage, put it this way:

As we take part in the rebuilding of Europe, we must remember that we are building world peace, not an American peace. Our cooperation with the free men of Europe must be founded on the basic principles of human dignity, and not on any theory that their way to freedom must be exactly the same as ours. . . . If we join in the task of reconstruction with courage, confidence, and good will, we shall learn—and teach—a lot. But we must start with a willingness to understand.

The strength now in place within the alliance has come, in good degree, because we started "with a willingness to understand." This experience should provide us with a foundation from which to project our understanding into the crises of the hour; to bring that understanding to bear on our internal stress and strain. Do this we must.

We came together in peril and in weakness. Confidence and strength have grown. We can yet achieve the great ends of the alliance—a better life, security, a real peace.

TELEVISION'S ROLE IN THE AMERICAN DEMOCRACY [9]

ROBERT W. SARNOFF [10]

Readers of REPRESENTATIVE AMERICAN SPEECHES: 1961-1962 will recall the addresses by Newton N. Minow and Frank Stanton which appeared in the section "Some Views on What Constitutes the Public Interest." In the editor's introduction to Mr. Stanton's lecture, reference was made to an address delivered by Robert W. Sarnoff, chairman of the board of the National Broadcasting Company, before the NBC Television and Radio Affiliates in Beverly Hills, California, on December 7, 1961. Coincidentally, this was also the date of Mr. Stanton's talk; and between them, these addresses represented the major replies by the industry to the persistent criticism of television as a sort of "wasteland." While the controversy is less acerbic than it was a year ago, it continues to be a newsworthy subject. And indeed the prospect of more severe governmental controls over broadcasting remains a matter of high concern to those who are committed to the principle of self-regulation.

Not all of the recent talks on television's role in society, however, have been in the defensive mood. Some have expressed positive affirmations of the distinctive function of broadcasting in a democratic state. One such address is the succinct statement of Robert W. Sarnoff before the Chicago World Trade Conference in Chicago, Illinois, on March 5, 1963. In this well-organized address, Mr. Sarnoff speaks of television's support of two basic concepts in American life: the free expression of opinion and the competitive free enterprise economy.

Students of public address will, moreover, appreciate the comments on the "Great Debates" over television in 1960, and on the projected plans for covering the 1964 campaign.

It is a high honor to be asked to speak before this knowledgeable audience, and I am grateful for your challenging invitation.

In approaching my assignment this evening, I am mindful of the many eminent men of government and industry who have occupied this rostrum in the past. This fills me with a sense of modesty, and brings to mind a remark made by another speaker

[9] Text furnished by Louis Hausman, vice president, general executive, National Broadcasting Company, with permission for this reprint.

[10] For biographical note, see Appendix.

on a different occasion. That, as you may recall, was when Sir Winston Churchill said of his personal friend and political foe, Clement Attlee: "He is a modest man with much to be modest about."

Since your last annual conference, the world has experienced both change and stalemate, and from the vantage point of the West, a normal complement of frustrations. There are fresh Indian graves in the Himalayas. Draining jungle wars continue in Southeast Asia. The wall still stands in Berlin, and Cuba remains a Communist fortress in our hemispheric seas. Even the rupture between the two Goliaths of world communism was prompted by *how*—not whether—to bury us.

Yet, the past year has also seen resolute strides by those nations with a commitment to freedom. In no section of the earth did we yield peoples or principles to communism, and we recently passed the eyeball test without a blink. In such critical outposts as Formosa and West Berlin, our posture is stronger, not weaker, than a year ago. In the contest beyond the earth's atmosphere, our astronauts brought us nearer to competitive parity with Russia; and our unmanned satellites, such as Telstar, Tiros and Relay, gave us clear leadership in global space communications.

But if I were to single out one event of paramount significance in the last year, it would be the performance of the American economy. Its continued resilience and strength, its ability to weather the worst market collapse in thirty-three years and then resume its forward progress, were more meaningful than any political event. There would be no free Berlins, no pacified Congos, if this powerful machine of individual and competitive enterprise were to falter and to fail.

In a recent, eloquent statement President Kennedy said:

We shall be judged more by what we do at home than what we preach abroad. Nothing we could do to help the developing countries would help them half as much as a booming United States economy. And nothing our opponents could do to encourage their own ambitions would encourage them half as much as a lagging United States economy.

It is to the indivisible goal of keeping our economy strong and our society free that I would like to address myself. And I hope it will not be regarded as immodest of me to suggest that the industry I represent—television—plays a role of decisive importance in stimulating economic growth and in reinforcing the strength of our democratic process.

Essentially, democracy is a union of two concepts. Television was born of both and supports both.

One is the concept of free expression which the late Judge Learned Hand characterized as "brave reliance upon free discussion." Rooted in tradition and sheltered by law, it holds that citizens of a democracy, given free access to knowledge, and freedom to discuss issues and views, can best judge their own interests and best guide their own destiny.

The other is the concept of a competitive free enterprise economy as best calculated to meet the needs of the individual and the nation. It has a dual premise: that open competition for public favor spurs the constant improvement of goods and services; and that the encouragement of mass demand sparks mass production, which, in turn, decreases the cost and increases the availability of these goods and services.

Both of these principles center on the individual as the master, not the servant, of the state; and both support the conviction that he can best realize his aspirations through ways of his own choosing. The opposite is true of the closed society, where the state is the master, controlling personal expression, political choice and all economic activity. The combat between the two systems is waged at every level—not only as a war of ideas, but as a war of economic strength.

Historically, free enterprise and democracy have nourished one another. The revolutions that led to the modern political systems of the West also fostered the rise of mercantile enterprise, the forerunner of the modern competitive free economy. Up to this day, those nations achieving the highest degree of consumer-oriented industrialization have also attained the most effective self-government.

Television's role in supporting this economic and political process is often obscured by the pervasive yet intimate nature of the service it offers. Most people have strong and subjective programing likes and dislikes. They might love the Beverly Hillbillies and be bored by the NBC Opera, or vice versa. They might become irritated by a commercial, or by a newscaster's comments on a subject where they have a preconceived judgment. The net effect—and this is perfectly natural—is that their personal preferences tend to eclipse a broader understanding of the medium's catalytic function in our society. I suggest the time is overdue for thoughtful Americans to begin evaluating the total dimension of the television service.

Its physical dimension is that of a service meeting so many needs and demands that in the United States in the last dozen years its circulation has grown from 10.5 million sets to nearly 59 million. The number of television stations, both commercial and noncommercial, has increased from 107 to 647. And television advertisers have expanded their annual expenditures from $332 million to $1.75 billion.

Our technology and programing have also provided substantial impetus to the growth of television abroad, in both the established and the emerging nations. From 1951 through 1961, the last year for which figures are available, the number of sets outside North America grew from 1.2 million to 54 million. At the current rate of growth, the total will probably exceed 74 million by the end of this year.

To understand television's economic role, one must first relate it to the nature of our economy. Economic growth, as you who live by trade are well aware, hinges on mounting production and a high level of employment, both stimulated by increased consumption. In a free economy, production expansion depends primarily on rising consumer demand; and in the mature American economy, rising demand requires, in addition to population growth, the continuous stimulation of consumer desires.

The primary stimulant is advertising, and among all forms of advertising, television has unique capabilities that power the American economy. For television is more than an advertising tool; like advertising, it creates demand, but with sight, sound, color and demonstration, it goes further and functions as a direct selling force. Its sales messages reach millions simultaneously, yet with the personal persuasion of one individual speaking to another in his home. With its ability to show not only what a product is but what it does, television has given American industry a powerful means of sustaining traditional consumer demands and developing new ones. It also has speeded and streamlined the distribution process. This is a contribution of particular value to our economy, where distribution cost is so important an element of end cost to consumers.

Television's sales impact has contributed to, and has been accompanied by, a marketing revolution in which the primary selling function has shifted from the dealer to the manufacturer. In the past, the dealer had the responsibility for developing the manufacturer's market. Today the manufacturer helps create the market for the dealer by speaking directly to his customers. He does this not only for consumer purchases but also, in increasing degree, for the sale of those products that are purchased for the ultimate user by someone else, such as plywood and plate glass for the home and aluminum for the automobile.

This ability of the manufacturer to engage in mass selling as well as mass production—whether of packaged goods on the shelves of supermarkets or automobiles or home appliances—has given our economy a highly effective means of continuous expansion.

It is against this perspective that criticism of an advertiser-supported television system should be considered—criticism which claims that the marketing function of the medium prevents it from properly discharging its program function in serving the audience. To my mind, there is no inconsistency, but a close parallel, between these functions. Both seek to engage the interests of large audiences, and this is a valid goal of a mass medium of entertainment and information, quite apart from its marketing role. Additionally, television recognizes minority interests and in doing so, it also serves the advertisers interested in such specialized audiences.

The debate over whether television strikes a proper balance between broad and specialized interests turns on a matter of degree. If there is such a thing as a perfect and ultimate balance, I will not claim that we have reached it. Yet this debate tends to lose sight of an undebatable fact—the basic contribution commercial television makes to the national economy; and the paramount need for national economic strength in preserving the institutions of our free society.

The premise of growth in the American economy is consumption—a principle underscored by the President in urging that billions of dollars be released to stimulate spending by private consumers, private investors and corporate enterprises.

Is the stimulation of private spending incompatible with meeting our public responsibilities? History argues otherwise, for as our consumption has increased, so has our allocation for essential services: billions of dollars for education, for social security benefits, for public welfare and old-age assistance, for highways and police and fire protection. While consuming more, we have paid the highest taxes in peacetime history, fought a war in Korea, given billions in foreign aid and maintained and strengthened our global defense structure, so vital to the survival of the free world.

Fortunately, we Americans need not choose between satisfying our personal desires and fulfilling our public obligations. We are spared such a choice by a rare, perhaps unique combination of blessings: our vast natural resources, our unsurpassed technological skill and a free and expanding economy based upon prosperity through consumption. Thus we can accomplish both goals. We can enjoy all the things that make work easier and leisure more fun—and at the same time meet the needs of society and the demands of security.

But we can sustain this formula, I believe, only if we maintain a protective and jealous attitude toward those institutions that make it possible. To do so, we must understand the nature of the political and economic forces that shape our environment. This is the function of free media of communications in a free society, anchored in the Jeffersonian conviction that men are inherently capable of making proper judgments when they are properly informed.

In this dimension of its service, television—alone of all media —is capable of bringing the sight and sound of great events of our time directly and instantaneously to nearly every man, woman and child in the nation, whether the occasion is a national political convention or the tense drama of a manned space shot. It can and does place viewers in direct contact with the pressure of diplomatic crisis in United Nations debate and the violence of controversy over segregation on the University of Mississippi campus. And beyond showing and describing events as they occur, television has pressed the nation's search for truth through its documentaries and its debates on major public issues, such as social welfare, state legislative processes, our diminishing water resources and legalized gambling.

As it has developed, television has properly intensified concentration on its journalistic function. For example, news and information programs account for more than 25 per cent of the total broadcast schedule of the NBC television network, and other networks and independent stations are also devoting increasing air time and creative effort to such presentation.

In addition to this concentration on equipping the citizen for more useful participation in society, the medium has forever altered the American political process. It has done so by presenting political candidates directly to the voters, culminating in the presidential campaign of 1960 and "The Great Debate."

This unrivaled opportunity to assess the two major candidates took place only after the nation's broadcasters had won a congressional respite from the equal time law. Ironically, once the 1960 campaign was concluded, they were forced back into the legal strait jacket that makes the debates impractical by requiring equal time on the air for all presidential candidates, no matter how quixotic their intent or meager their support.

I am hopeful that before the 1964 election campaign begins, the Congress will relieve the public and the broadcasters of this restriction. An early start has already been made in this direction. Chairman Harris of the House Interstate and Foreign Commerce Committee has introduced a resolution for suspension of the equal time restriction to permit the 1964 presidential and vice presidential candidates to meet in face-to-face debate on the air. Yesterday, I testified in Washington in support of this proposal. However, I strongly urged that the Congress go further by eliminating, completely and permanently, the equal time restraint which operates against the free flow of information in the crucial area of political judgment and choice. Given this freedom, and the responsibility broadcasters have already demonstrated in providing full and fair coverage, television could serve the voters at the state and local levels as it has served them nationally.

While conceding the immense value of the four confrontations of 1960 in exposing the presidential candidates to intimate public scrutiny, some thoughtful analysts hold that they were neither "great" nor "debates." They argue that the format—which the candidates themselves helped develop—did not permit sufficient analysis of the issues for the guidance of the voter or, in fact, expose adequately what the issues were. This point of view is far from unanimous and addresses itself to method rather than principle, but I believe it is worthy of serious consideration.

Accordingly, in the expectation that the law will again be changed to permit debates between presidential candidates, we should start now to refine the format of these televised encounters, seeking even more effective ways of assisting the American voter to make an informed choice.

As a major step in this direction, the National Broadcasting Company has enlisted the aid of the American Political Science Association, the nation's foremost professional organization devoted to the study of government, politics and public affairs. I am pleased to announce that this distinguished organization has agreed to conduct an independent study, under a grant from NBC, to devise the best possible forms and procedures for televised political debates.

The association has made many significant contributions to more effective government—its most recent, a widely acclaimed orientation course for new members of Congress, an innovation that is likely to become a Washington tradition.

It has selected a seven-man study group of distinguished political scientists and communications experts to carry out the project proposed by NBC. The group will be headed by the association's president, Dr. Carl J. Friedrich, Eaton Professor of the Science of Government at Harvard University.

NBC's only participation in this study will be to underwrite the cost and provide necessary and basic information, including tape or film recordings of the 1960 debates. Whatever recommendations are arrived at will be the group's own, the result of careful, scholarly deliberation. By starting at this early date, the group will be able to present its findings well in advance of the 1964 presidential campaign. I am confident that its proposals will be a major contribution to our democratic process.

Beyond equal time, we face the broader issue of whether any communuications medium can effectively serve as an instrument of democracy if its freedom is curtailed. Today, television is fettered in many areas of journalistic enterprise. It cannot go wherever the public goes—into the halls of Congress, into public committee meetings of the House of Representatives, into most courtrooms.

Television does not seek this right in order to make a theater of serious forums, and it recognizes the need for care and restraint. I emphasize, however, that wherever the public can attend, television should also be permitted to attend, so that it can serve as the eyes and ears of *all* the people. The right to witness public business should not be confined only to those whom the hearing room will hold, when television can bring the public business to everyone.

Wherever it serves, whether entertaining or informing, television functions best in a climate of freedom. It is paradoxical that in the area of news coverage, where television's need for freedom is recognized by all, restrictions on coverage should be placed through the equal time penalty and the limitations on access. And it is even more paradoxical that among the strongest champions of television's freedom to report information and controversy without restraints are those who urge Government restrictions on television entertainment. They would erect a double standard—one for information programs, another for entertainment programs—failing to recognize that freedom is indivisible. Would magazines and newspapers be free if only their news columns were unmolested, if the choice and content of features and fiction were subject to Government influence, direct or indirect? But this is all part of that democratic process in which television was conceived. Often we who have the responsibility for guiding this service are accused of excessive sensitivity toward criticism. I assure you we welcome responsible criticism and take it seriously. It would be fatal to television's development if it were to operate in a vacuum of indifference and ignorance.

What we seek is understanding of the total dimension of our television service—its contribution to the political processes that keep us free, its impact upon the economic forces which keep America strong.

These essential and inseparable functions of political and economic freedom are the source of this nation's vitality and strength. Our capacity to support the arch of democracy both at home and around the world can be limited only if these freedoms are limited. It will grow only as we succeed in keeping them unencumbered. Thank you.

A NEW DEPARTURE IN COMMUNICATION

A CONVERSATION WITH THE PRESIDENT [1]

JOHN F. KENNEDY [2]

It is not easy for a head of state, whether in America or elsewhere, to report informally to a nation-wide audience. The physical setup of microphones and lights and cameras introduces a certain contrived element; and the simple fact that a leader is in public view, that his supporters and critics alike are sensitively alert to the implications of what he says, especially during unguarded moments, places the perform-ance in a mold that is something less than flexible. It is not surprising therefore, that leaders search for a format that will insure the freest measure of communication in an atmosphere that will radiate warmth, directness, and spontaneity.

Some men have been uncommonly successful in making a pre-pared speech on a grave theme sound like a relatively informal re-port. Franklin D. Roosevelt did it. His first fireside chat on March 12, 1933, was so written and delivered as to make his radio listeners feel that he was talking over a problem with them in the quiet of their living rooms. He explained the reason for the bank holiday and the steps the Government was taking to meet the emergency and pre-vent its recurrence. Thanking the public for its cooperation in meet-ing the crisis, he then appealed for their continued help in restoring confidence in the financial structure. It was all said and done with such simplicity and directness that it seemed much like a sustained conver-sation in which the listeners had asked the questions and he had supplied the comforting answers.

In recent years the formal speech has been used more specifically for the announcement and explanation of imminent crises. Reports to the nation on the less dramatic happenings are made largely through press conferences. But the press conference has some critical short-comings, chief of which is its stereotyped form. Many questions are asked on topics covering an infinite spectrum and only short answers

[1] Transcript furnished by Pierre Salinger, press secretary to the President, with per-mission for this reprint. William H. Lawrence's comments and questions are reprinted by permission of Kay Murphy, manager of literary rights division, American Broadcasting Company; George Herman's, by permission of Josef C. Dine, director of information and special services, CBS News, Columbia Broadcasting System; Sander Vanocur's, by permis-sion of Myron I. Roth, legal department, National Broadcasting Company.

[2] For biographical note, see Appendix.

at best are given. The over-all effect is a composite of opinions and facts that may make satisfactory newspaper copy, but scarcely gives the average viewer-listener a unified impression of what is going on in governmental circles. On the other hand, the conference does provide an authentic specimen of "live rhetoric"; the morning's transcript indicates, often mercilessly, what a man said while thinking on his feet, even to the occasional grammatical and syntactical slips which doubtless cause subsequent embarrassment.

Recently, interviews and reports have been used extensively to educate the public on current events. On November 28, 1962, David Schoenbrun, chief Washington correspondent of the Columbia Broadcasting System, interviewed Secretary of State Dean Rusk on the changing patterns in world affairs. It was an informative and satisfying sixty-minute program. Over a nation-wide radio and television hook-up on February 6, 1963, Defense Secretary Robert S. McNamara gave an elaborate report on the Cuban situation, refuting the claims of the critics that the Soviet military build-up on the island was continuing. According to *Time* magazine, Secretary McNamara's "manner was that of a professor patiently explaining a simple matter to a slightly backward class."

On December 16, 1962, three news representatives interviewed President Kennedy at the White House for ninety minutes. The conversation was then edited slightly, reducing it to an hour for presentation over a national radio-television hook-up on the following evening, December 17. In a pattern of unhurried reflection, the President responded to questions put by William H. Lawrence of the American Broadcasting Company, George Herman of the Columbia Broadcasting System, and Sander Vanocur of the National Broadcasting Company. It resulted in one of the most effective communications yet made by the President.

The interview gave illuminating insights into the way a leader—confident, knowledgeable, and eager to share his thoughts and feelings with an audience—faces tough decisions and arrives at judgments and actions. But the program offered more than the revelation of a personality, important as that is. It also underscored issues on which the public needs continually, even repetitively, to get information. Although the interview came under some criticism for a "lack of hard questioning," the frank discussion of the Cuban crisis alone showed that the tough topics were not bypassed. "When the program came to an end," wrote Jack Gould, television critic of the New York *Times*, "the viewer truly had a sense of having shared the President's perspective on the world and nation." Here, indeed, was an hour of revealing talk, of effective rocking chair rhetoric. Provided the questioning is frank and fearless, and the program is free from any kind of control or management, the conversation offers inviting possibilities for education and political persuasion.

MR. LAWRENCE: As you look back upon your first two years in office, sir, has your experience in the office matched your expectations? You had studied a good deal the power of the presidency, the methods of its operations. How has this worked out as you saw it in advance?

THE PRESIDENT: Well, I think in the first place the problems are more difficult than I had imagined they were. Secondly, there is a limitation upon the ability of the United States to solve these problems. We are involved now in the Congo in a very difficult situation. We have been unable to secure an implementation of the policy which we have supported. We are involved in a good many other areas. We are trying to see if a solution can be found to the struggle between Pakistan and India, with whom we want to maintain friendly relations. Yet they are unable to come to an agreement. There is a limitation, in other words, upon the power of the United States to bring about solutions.

I think our people get awfully impatient and maybe fatigued and tired, and saying "We have been carrying this burden for seventeen years; can we lay it down?" We can't lay it down, and I don't see how we are going to lay it down in this century.

So that I would say that the problems are more difficult than I had imagined them to be. The responsibilities placed on the United States are greater than I imagined them to be, and there are greater limitations upon our ability to bring about a favorable result than I had imagined them to be. And I think that is probably true of anyone who becomes President, because there is such a difference between those who advise or speak or legislate, and between the man who must select from the various alternatives proposed and say that this shall be the policy of the United States. It is much easier to make the speeches than it is to finally make the judgments, because unfortunately your advisers are frequently divided. If you take the wrong course, and on occasion I have, the President bears the burden of the responsibility quite rightly. The advisers may move on to new advice.

MR. LAWRENCE: Well, Mr. President, that brings up a point that has always interested me. How does a President go about making a decision, like Cuba, for example?

THE PRESIDENT: The most recent one was hammered out really on policy and decision over a period of five or six days. During that period, the fifteen people more or less who were directly consulted frequently changed their view, because whatever action we took had so many disadvantages to it, and each action we took raised the prospect that it might escalate with the Soviet Union into a nuclear war. Finally, however, I think a general consensus developed, and [it] certainly seemed after all alternatives were examined, that the course of action that we finally adopted was the right one.

Now, when I talked to members of the Congress, several of them suggested a different alternative, when we confronted them on that Monday with the evidence. My feeling is that if they had gone through the five-day period we had gone through in looking at the various alternatives, the advantages and disadvantages of action, they probably would have come out the same way that we did. I think that we took the right one. If we had had to act on Wednesday in the first twenty-four hours, I don't think probably we would have chosen as prudently as we finally did, a quarantine against the use of offensive weapons.

In addition, that had much more power than we first thought it did, because I think the Soviet Union was very reluctant to have us stop ships which carried with them a good deal of their highly secret and sensitive material. One of the reasons I think that the Soviet Union withdrew the IL-28's was because we were carrying on very intensive low-level photography. Now, no one would have guessed, probably, that that would have been such a harassment. Mr. Castro could not permit us to indefinitely continue widespread flights over his island at two hundred feet every day, and yet he knew if he shot down one of our planes, that then it would bring back a much more serious reprisal on him. So it is very difficult to always make judgments here about what the effect will be of our decisions on other countries. In this case, it seems to me that we did pick the right one; in Cuba of 1961 we picked the wrong one.

MR. HERMAN: I would like to go back to the question of the consensus and your relationship to the consensus. You have said and the Constitution says that the decision can be made only by the President.

THE PRESIDENT: Well, you know that old story about Abraham Lincoln and the Cabinet. He said, "All in favor, say 'aye,'" and the whole Cabinet voted "aye," and then "All opposed, no," and Lincoln voted "no" and he said, "The vote is no." So that naturally the Constitution places the responsibility on the President. There was some disagreement with the course we finally adopted, but the course we finally adopted had the advantage of permitting other steps if this one was unsuccessful. In other words, we were starting in a sense at a minimum place. Then if that were unsuccessful, we could have gradually stepped it up until we had gone into a much more massive action, which might have become necessary if the first step had been unsuccessful. I would think that the majority finally came to accept that, though at the beginning there was a much sharper division. And after all, this was very valuable, because the people who were involved had particular responsibilities of their own; Mr. McNamara, secretary of defense, therefore had to advise me on the military capacity of the United States in that area, the secretary of state, who had to advise on the attitude of the OAS and NATO. So that in my opinion, the majority came to accept the course we finally took. It made it much easier. In the Cuba of 1961, the advice of those who were brought in on the executive branch was also unanimous, and the advice was wrong. And I was responsible. So that finally it comes down that no matter how many advisers you have, frequently they are divided, and the President must finally choose.

The other point is something that President Eisenhower said to me on January 19. He said, "There are no easy matters that will ever come to you as President. If they are easy, they will be settled at a lower level." So that the matters that come to you as President are always the difficult matters, and matters that carry with them large implications. So this contributes to some of the burdens of the office of the presidency, which other Presidents have commented on.

MR. VANOCUR: Mr. President, during the Cuban crisis, there was some problem that you are apparently familiar with and bored with by now, about the possibility of a President talking in very private and secret conversations with his advisers, and that somehow leaking out. Do you think that this is going to inhibit the free, frank flow of advice that every President has to have?

THE PRESIDENT: No. I think it is unfortunate there are that sort of conversations, but there are what, 1,300 reporters accredited to the White House alone, there are I suppose 100 or 150 people who are familiar with what goes on in the Security Council meeting in one way or another. You have the people who are actually there. Then you have got the others who are given instructions as a result of the decisions there, and I suppose people do talk. And then as I said at the time of the Cuban disaster in April of 1961 that success has a hundred fathers and defeat is an orphan. I suppose when something goes well, there is more tendency to talk at all levels, and frequently the reports are inaccurate. I would say the security is pretty good at the National Security Council. It is unfortunate when it is breached.

MR. VANOCUR: Is it true that during your first year, sir, you would get on the phone personally to the State Department and try to get a response to some inquiry that had been made?

THE PRESIDENT: Yes, I still do that when I can, because I think there is a great tendency in Government to have papers stay on desks too long, and it seems to me that is really one function. After all, the President can't administer a department, but at least he can be a stimulant.

MR. VANOCUR: Do you recall any response that you received from somebody who was not suspecting a phone call in the State Department, any specific response somebody made to you?

THE PRESIDENT: No, they always respond. They always say yes. It takes a little while to get it. You know, after I met Mr. Khrushchev in Vienna and they gave us an *aide mémoire,* it took me many weeks to get our answer out through the State Department, coordinated with the British, the French and the Germans. It took much too long. Now, it seems to me we have been able to speed it up, but this is a constant problem in various departments. There are so many interests that are involved in any decision. No matter whether the decision is about Africa or Asia, it involves the Europe desk, it involves the desk of the place, it involves the Defense Department, it might involve the CIA, it frequently involves the Treasury, it might involve the World Bank, it involves the United Nations Delegation. So it seems to me that one of the functions of the President is to try to have it move with more speed. Otherwise you can wait while the world collapses.

MR. VANOCUR: You once said that you were reading more and enjoying it less. Are you still as avid a newspaper reader, [or] magazine—I remember those of us who traveled with you on the campaign, a magazine wasn't safe around you.

THE PRESIDENT: Oh, yes. No, no, I think it is invaluable, even though it may cause you—it is never pleasant to be reading things that are not agreeable news, but I would say that it is an invaluable arm of the presidency, to check really on what is going on in the Administration, and more things come to my attention that cause me concern or give me information. So I would think that Mr. Khrushchev operating a totalitarian system which has many advantages as far as being able to move in secret, and all the rest—there is a terrific disadvantage not having the abrasive quality of the press applied to you daily, to an Administration, even though we never like it, and even though we wish they didn't write it, and even though we disapprove, there isn't any doubt that we could not do the job at all in a free society without a very, very active press.

Now, on the other hand, the press has the responsibility not to distort things for political purposes, not to just take some news in order to prove a political point. It seems to me their obligation is to be as tough as they can on the Administration but do it in a way which is directed towards getting as close to the truth as they can get and not merely because of some political motivation.

MR. LAWRENCE: Mr. President, in the light of the election returns, which at the congressional level at least were certainly a defeat for the Republican hopes, how do you measure your chances for significant success domestically in the Congress just ahead?

THE PRESIDENT: Well, I think we will be about in the same position as the last two years. As I say, what we have that is controversial will be very closely contested.

MR. LAWRENCE: Did the complexion of the House change a little bit by these shifts?

THE PRESIDENT: I would say slightly against us more than it was. We are not in quite as good shape as we were for the last two years, but we are about where we were the last two years, which means that every vote will be three or four votes either way, winning or losing.

MR. LAWRENCE: Do you have a very crucial vote at the outset on this Rules Committee fight again, do you think?

THE PRESIDENT: I hope that the Rules Committee is kept to its present number, because we can't function if it isn't. We are through if we lose—if they try to change the Rules. Nothing controversial in that case would come to the floor of the Congress. Our whole program in my opinion would be emasculated.

MR. LAWRENCE: As a young congressman, sir, you voted to impose a two-term limitation on Presidents. Now that you have held the office for a while, and also observed its effect on President Eisenhower's second term, would you repeat that vote, even if the amendment did not apply to yourself?

THE PRESIDENT: Yes, I would. I would. I know the conditions were special in 1947, but I think eight years is enough, and I am not sure that a President—in my case if I were re-elected—that you are at such a disadvantage. There are not many jobs. That is not the power of the presidency, patronage, at all. They are filled in the first months. Most of those jobs belong to the members of the Congress, anyway. So patronage is not a factor. I think there are many other powers of the presidency that run in the second term as well as the first.

MR. VANOCUR: Mr. President, on that point —

THE PRESIDENT: The fact of the matter is President Eisenhower has great influence today in the Republican party, and therefore in the country, and has great influence in foreign policy, and he does not even hold office. In some ways his influence is greater to some degree. So that the same is really also true of President Truman and President Hoover. I don't think that it depends—the influence of a President is still substantial in his second term. Though I haven't had a second term, I think it is.

MR. VANOCUR: Mr. President, on that point, much of your program still remains to be passed by the Congress. There are some people who say that you either do it in the next two years, or it won't be done, should you be elected to a second term. Do you share that point of view?

THE PRESIDENT: No. In the first place, I think we have got a lot by. I was looking at what we set out to do in January of

1961 the other day, and on taxes, and on social security, welfare changes, area redevelopment, minimum wage, Peace Corps, the Alliance for Progress, the Disarmament Agency and strengthening the defenses and strengthening our space program. We did all those things—the trade bill—not perhaps to the extent in every case of our original proposal, but substantial progress. I think we can do some more the next two years. I would think there are going to be new problems if I were reelected in 1965, and I don't think—I don't look at the second term as necessarily a decline. I don't think that at all. In fact, I think you know much more about the position. It is a tremendous change to go from being a senator to being President. In the first months, it is very difficult. But I have no reason to believe that a President with the powers of this office and the responsibilities placed on it—if he has a judgment that some things need to be done, I think he can do it just as well the second time as the first, depending of course on the make-up of the Congress. The fact is I think the Congress looks more powerful sitting here than it did when I was there in the Congress. But that is because when you are in Congress you are one of a hundred in the Senate or one of 435 in the House. So that the power is so divided. But from here I look at a Congress, and I look at the collective power of the Congress, particularly the bloc action, and it is a substantial power.

MR. VANOCUR: Mr. President, power like charity, as you have noted, begins at home, and you seem to have one view of what we need to do at home, and Congress seems to have another view. A lot of money will be appropriated for defense and national security, but there is a certain reluctance to devote money to another form of capital investment, education, and other things like that at home. Is it purely a question of money, or is this religious thing really going to make it impossible for you to get an education act passed?

THE PRESIDENT: Well, education—it is certainly the question of how the funds will be distributed; how they will be shared is one of the factors. The integration question is another matter which comes into it. I think—you know, Thomas Jefferson once said to expect the people to be ignorant and free is to expect what never was and never will be. Here we are going to have twice as many people trying to go to college in 1970 as 1960.

That means we have to build as many buildings in ten years as we built the whole 160 years of our country's history. Then you have got these millions of young boys and girls who are dropping out of school, who are unskilled, at a time when unskilled—when skilled labor is needed, and not unskilled. So we need money for vocational training to train them in skills, to retrain workers, to provide assistance funds for colleges, and then to provide assistance to those who are going to get doctorates, higher advanced in engineering, science and mathematics. We have a severe shortage there. And yet we are asking for space, defense and all the rest. The Soviet Union is concentrating on this. So all this requires funds, but it is all in controversy. Some people feel the Federal Government should play no role, and yet the Federal Government, since the Land Grant Act and back to the Northwest Ordinance, has played a major role. I think the Federal Government has a great responsibility in the field of education. We can't maintain our strength industrially, militarily, scientifically, socially, without very well-educated citizenry. And I think the Federal Government has a role to play. So we are going to send up a program. Unfortunately, because of the fact, as you mentioned, and other reasons, we have come close to getting assistance to education passed, but we have not been successful.

MR. LAWRENCE: Mr. President, is your problem of getting an education bill through this year made more difficult by the events at Oxford, Mississippi, and the use of Federal troops there?

THE PRESIDENT: Yes, I think so.

MR. LAWRENCE: How will you combat this new—

THE PRESIDENT: Well, as I say, this is a case of where we have come very close, and President Eisenhower came close, and we came close once—we got a bill through the House, through the Senate, almost through the House, and we didn't get it. Then another try for higher education through the Senate and the House, and then it failed—the conference failed. Now, Oxford, Mississippi, which has made this whole question of the Federal Government and education more sensitive—in some parts of the country I suppose that is going to be a factor against us. I don't really know what other role they would expect the President of the United States to play. The court made up of southern judges determined it was according to the Constitutiton that Mr. Meredith go to the University of Mississippi. The governor of Mississippi opposed it, and there was rioting against Mr. Meredith, which endangered his life. We sent in marshals, and after all, 150 or 160 marshals were wounded in one way or another out of four or five hundred, and at least three fourths of the marshals were from the South themselves. Then we sent in troops when it appeared that the marshals were going to be overrun. I don't think that anybody who looks at the situation can think we could possibly do anything else. We couldn't possibly do anything else. But on the other hand, I recognize that it has caused a lot of bitterness against me and against the national Government in Mississippi and other parts, and though they expect me to carry out my oath under the Constitution—and that is what we are going to do. But it does make it more difficult to pass an education bill. But I think we shouldn't penalize this great resource of our youth for all these reasons. Instead, we ought to do the job and get these schools built, these teachers compensated, and higher education available to all these boys and girls—every time I drive around the country, that is all you see, are six- and seven- and eight- and nine-year-old children who are going to be pouring into our schools and colleges, and every governor will tell you that is his major problem, providing educational facilities, where the national Government has a responsibility.

MR. VANOCUR: Do you think we could turn for a moment to this subject of the President's responsibility in foreign affairs? Now, when some congressmen disagreed with your course of action over Cuba on that Monday, the responsibility you have by the Constitution in this is very clear, but in domestic matters, the responsibility is divided. How do you use the presidency in Theodore Roosevelt's phrase "the bully pulpit," to move these men who really are kind of barons and sovereigns in their own right up there on the Hill? Have you any way to move them toward a course of action which you think is imperative?

THE PRESIDENT: Well, the Constitution and the development of the Congress all give advantage to delay. It is very easy to defeat a bill in the Congress. It is much more difficult to pass one. To go through a committee, say the Ways and Means Committee of the House, subcommittee and get a majority vote, the full committee and get a majority vote, go to the Rules

Committee and get a rule, go to the floor of the House and get a majority, start over again in the Senate, subcommittee and full committee, and in the Senate there is unlimited debate, so you can never bring a matter to a vote if there is enough determination on the part of the opponents, even if they are a minority, to go through the Senate with the bill. And then unanimously get a conference between the House and Senate to adjust the bill, or if one member objects, to have it go back through the Rules Committee, back through the Congress, and have this done on a controversial piece of legislation where powerful groups are opposing it—that is an extremely difficult task. So that the struggle of a President who has a program to move it through the Congress, particularly when the seniority system may place particular individuals in key positions who may be wholly unsympathetic to your program, and may be, even though they are members of your own party, in political opposition to the President—this is a struggle which every President who has tried to get a program through has had to deal with. After all, Franklin Roosevelt was elected by the largest majority in history in 1936, and he got his worst defeat a few months afterwards in the Supreme Court bill [which was designed to allow reorganization of the Supreme Court, but was immediately dubbed the "Court-packing" bill].

So that they are two separate offices and two separate powers, the Congress and the presidency. There is bound to be conflict, but they must cooperate to the degree that is possible. But that is why no President's program is ever put in. The only time a President's program is put in quickly and easily is when the program is insignificant. But if it is significant and affects important interests and is controversial, therefore, then there is a fight, and the President is never wholly successful.

MR. VANOCUR: Mr. President, which is the better part of wisdom, to take a bill which is completely emasculated, that you had great interest in and accept it, or accept its defeat in the hope of building up public support for it at a later time?

THE PRESIDENT: Well, I would say given the conditions you described, I think it would be better to accept the defeat, but usually what has happened, and what has happened to us in the last two years, a good many of our bills passed in reasonable condition, not the way we sent them up, but after all, the Congress has its own will and its own feelings and its own judgment, and they are close to the people. The whole House of Representatives has just been elected, so that it is quite natural that they will have a different perspective than I may have. So I would say that [what] we ought to do is to do the best we can. But if it is completely emasculated, then there is no sense in having a shadow of success and not the substance.

MR. LAWRENCE: Mr. President, in the exercise of presidential power, and I think perhaps the best-known case and the most widely talked about was your rollback of steel prices after they had been announced by the steel companies, some people have suggested that in retrospect that perhaps you would not have acted so vigorously. Is there any truth in this suggestion?

THE PRESIDENT: I must say it would have been a very serious situation though I don't like to rake over old fires—I think it would have been a serious situation if I had not attempted with all my influence to try to get a rollback, because there was an issue of good faith involved. The steel union had accepted the most limited settlement that they had had since the end of the Second World War. They had accepted it three or four months ahead. They did it in part, I think, because I said that we could not afford another inflationary spiral, that it would affect our competitive position abroad, so they signed up. Then when their last contract was signed, which was the Friday or Saturday before, then steel put its prices up immediately. It seemed to me that the question of good faith was involved, and that if I had not attempted, after asking the unions to accept the noninflationary settlement, if I had not attempted to use my influence to have the companies hold their prices stable, I think the union could have rightfully felt that they had been misled. In my opinion it would have endangered the whole bargaining between labor and management, would have made it impossible for us to exert any influence from the public point of view in the future on these great labor-management disputes which do affect the public interest. So I have no regrets. The fact is, we were successful.

Now, supposing we had tried and made a speech about it, and then failed. I would have thought that would have been an awful setback to the office of the presidency. Now, I just think, looking back on it, that I would not change it at all. There is no sense in raising hell, and then not being successful. There is no sense in putting the office of the presidency on the line on an issue, and then being defeated. Now, an unfortunate repercussion of that was the strong feeling that the Government might interfere in a good many labor-management matters, or that it might interfere in the whole question of the free enterprise system. It was regrettable that that general conclusion was drawn in this particular incident. Given the problem that I had on that Tuesday night, I must say I think we had to do everything we could to get it reversed.

MR. LAWRENCE: Mr. President, your predecessor, President Eisenhower, in his farewell message to the people just before he left office, warned of the dangers of a possible military-industrial complex that might threaten the very nature of the democracy. Have you felt this threat at all while you were in office?

THE PRESIDENT: Well, it seems to me there was probably more in that feeling some months ago than I would say today. Of course, every time you cancel a weapons system, it affects a good many thousands of people, the interests of a community, the interests of members of Congress, the interests of the state, and we have had a long fight, for example, over the B-70, which we have felt is a weapon that isn't worth the money we would have to put into it. But it is a very difficult struggle with the Congress. Twice now Congress has appropriated the money for the program; twice we have not spent that money. But I must say as of today I don't feel that the pressure on us is excessive.

MR. LAWRENCE: Well, I was particularly attracted, sir, by an advertisement, a two-page color advertisement this week in one of the national magazines, for the Project Skybolt missile.

THE PRESIDENT: Yes, I saw the ad.

MR. LAWRENCE: And it claimed only successes for the missile. It mentioned no failures, though you had pointed out five, and it said that this system would save billions of dollars in tax dollars if developed. Now, did you regard that as pressure on you?

THE PRESIDENT: Well, I think it was an attempt to influence our decision. I see nothing wrong with that. The fact of the matter is that this Skybolt is very essential to the future of the Douglas Company. There are thousands of jobs that are involved. There are a good many people in the United States who feel that this program would be useful, and of course the British feel very strongly about it. So I think the ad was an attempt to bring what the Douglas company feels are the facts to my attention, to Mr. McNamara's, in a different form. In fact, I saw that ad today. The only thing that we ought to point out is we are talking about $2.5 billion to build a weapon to hang on our B-52's, when we already have billions invested in Polaris, and Minuteman. We are talking about developing now Titan III and other missiles. There is just a limit to how much we need, as well as how much we can afford to have a successful deterrent. Your submarines in the ocean, we have Minutemen on the ground, we have B-52 planes, we still have some B-47's, we have the tactical forces in Europe. I would say when we start to talk about the megatonnage we could bring into a nuclear war, we are talking about annihilation. How many times do you have to hit a target with nuclear weapons? That is why when we are talking about spending this $2.5 billion, we don't think that we are going to get $2.5 billion worth of national security. Now, I know there are others who disagree, but that is our feeling.

MR. HERMAN: As we move forward technically, Mr. President, new weapons systems and new devices which may be vital to the future of the country seem to get more and more expensive, and to involve more and more thousands of men working on them. Are we coming to a point where perhaps we are going to be so involved that once you start a new weapons system into the works, you will be almost bound to continue it, because to discontinue it would dislocate the economy, put thousands out of work again, and so forth?

THE PRESIDENT: Well, that is a problem. In addition, these systems are always two or three or four times more expensive than they look like they are going to be. One of the problems that we have now is the question of whether we should begin to put out the Nike-Zeus system, which is an antimissile missile system around this country. We hope sometime to develop a system which will permit us to fire a missile at a missile coming towards us and destroy it, and thereby prevent an atomic attack on the United States. But it will cost billions. There is no sense going ahead until that system is perfected. Some think now is the time, but we are going to wait for a further period of investigation. But there isn't any doubt that if you don't build the B-70 or you don't build the Skybolt, this involves thousands of jobs, and the welfare of communities, and this is one of our toughest problems. On the other hand, we can't have our defense budget go out of sight. We are now spending $52 billion a year, which is a tremendous amount of money, and we could go up to $60 or $65 billion if we didn't tighten as much as we can.

MR. HERMAN: Did the Nike-Zeus program get any impetus from Mr. Khrushchev's boast that he can hit a fly in the sky at the moment?

THE PRESIDENT: He might hit a fly, but whether he could hit a thousand flies with decoys—you see, every missile that comes might have four or five missiles in it, or would appear to be missiles, and the radar screen has to pick those out and hit them going thousands of miles an hour, and select which one is the real missile and which are the decoys, when there might be hundreds of objects coming through the air. That is a terribly difficult task. You can hit one. What you are trying to do is shoot a bullet with a bullet. Now, if you have a thousand bullets coming at you, that is a terribly difficult task which we have not mastered yet, and I don't think he has. The offense has the advantage.

MR. HERMAN: You think he has mastered the art of hitting one bullet?

THE PRESIDENT: Yes; so have we.

MR. LAWRENCE: Mr. President, you spoke the other day of the dangers and difficulties of slow communications between here and the Soviet Union, as it exhibited itself during the Cuban crisis. I suppose this would be an even graver problem if your radar screen were to pick up missiles or at least what appeared to be missiles in any substantial number?

THE PRESIDENT: Yes. Well, there is—one of the arguments for the continuation of the airplane is that if you picked up missiles coming toward you, you could have your planes take off and be in the air. Then if it proved to be a false alarm, then you could call them back. For missiles, you can't do that, and the President might have to make a judgment in a fifteen-minute period, and the information would be incomplete. You recall that incident where the moon came up, and it appeared to be a whole variety of missiles coming in. Of course, it was picked up several years ago. I think that is oversimplified. The fact of the matter is that the United States could wait quite long because we have missiles in hardened sites, and those missiles, even if there was a missile attack on the United States—those missiles could still be fired and destroy the Soviet Union, and so could the Polaris submarine missiles. So that I don't think there is a danger that we would fire based on incomplete and inaccurate information, because we were only given five or six minutes to make a judgment. I think the Polaris alone permits us to wait to make sure that we are going to have sufficient in hand that he knows that we could destroy the Soviet Union. Actually that is the purpose of the deterrent. Once he fires his missiles, it is all over anyway, because we are going to have sufficient resources to fire back at him to destroy the Soviet Union. When that day comes, and there is a massive exchange, then that is the end, because you are talking about Western Europe, the Soviet Union, the United States, of 150 million fatalities in the first eighteen hours. Now, you could go on, if everybody aimed at cities in order to have as many killed as possible in all these communities with all the weapons you could fire, you could kill, and you might be having more fire. So that the nuclear age is a very dangerous period, and that is why I frequently read these speeches about how we must do this and that. But I think they ought to just look at what we are talking about.

MR. LAWRENCE: How urgent is this need for quicker communication between here and the Soviet Union?

THE PRESIDENT: It is desirable. It is not—if he fires his missiles at us, it is not going to do any good for us to have a telephone at the Kremlin. But I do think that—and ask him whether it is really true. But I do think that it is better that we should be quicker than we now are. It took us some hours in the Cuban matter, and I think that communication is important. In addition to the communications with the Kremlin, we have very poor communications to a good deal of Latin America, and we don't know what is going on there very frequently. So we are trying to improve our communications all around the world, because that knowledge is so vital to an effective decision.

MR. VANOCUR: Mr. President, have you noted since you have been in office that this terrible responsibility for the fate of mankind has, notwithstanding the differences that divide you—has drawn you and Mr. Khrushchev somewhat closer in this joint sense of responsibility? He seems to betray it, especially in his speech to the Supreme Soviet earlier.

THE PRESIDENT: I think in that speech this week he showed his awareness of the nuclear age, but of course, the Cuban effort has made it more difficult for us to carry out any successful negotiations, because this was an effort to materially change the balance of power, it was done in secret, steps were taken really to deceive us by every means they could, and they were planning in November to open to the world the fact that they had these missiles so close to the United States; not that they were intending to fire them, because if they were going to get into a nuclear struggle, they have their own missiles in the Soviet Union. But it would have politically changed the balance of power. It would have appeared to, and appearances contribute to reality. So it is going to be some time before it is possible for us to come to any real understandings with Mr. Khrushchev. But I do think his speech shows that he realizes how dangerous a world we live in. The real problem is the Soviet desire to expand their power and influence. If Mr. Khrushchev would concern himself with the real interests of the people of the Soviet Union, that they have a higher standard of living, to protect his own security, there is no real reason why the United States and the Soviet Union, separated by so many thousands of miles of land and water, both rich countries, both with very energetic people, should not be able to live in peace. But it is this constant determination which the Chinese show in the most militant form, and which the Soviets also have shown, that they will not settle for that kind of a peaceful world, but must settle for a Communist world. That is what makes the real danger; the combination of these two systems in conflict around the world in a nuclear age is what makes the sixties so dangerous.

MR. VANOCUR: Ambassador Kennan, who has some knowledge of the Soviet Union, wrote in one of his recent books that what you are dealing with here is a conditioned state of mind, that there is no misunderstanding here, that the only thing the Soviets really understand is when you present them with a set of facts and say to them, "This is what we are going to do." This they understand. Have you found that there is any way to break through to Mr. Khrushchev, to make him really aware that you are quite sincere and determined about what you say, sir, or is this a total—

THE PRESIDENT: Well, it is difficult. I think, looking back on Cuba, what is of concern is the fact that both governments were so far out of contact, really. I don't think that we expected that he would put the missiles in Cuba, because it would have seemed such an imprudent action for him to take, as it was later proved. Now, he obviously must have thought that he could do it in secret and that the United States would accept it. So that he did not judge our intentions accurately.

Well, now, if you look at the history of this century, where World War I really came through a series of misjudgments of the intentions of others; certainly World War II, where Hitler thought that he could seize Poland, that the British might not fight, and if they fought, after the defeat of Poland they might not continue to fight; Korea, where obviously the North Koreans did not think we are going to come in; and Korea, when we did not think the Chinese were going to come in—when you look at all those misjudgments which brought on war, and then you see the Soviet Union and the United States so far separated in their beliefs, we believing in a world of independent sovereign and different diverse nations, they believing in a monolithic Communist world, and you put the nuclear equation into that struggle, that is what makes this, as I said before, such a dangerous time, and that we must proceed with firmness and also with the best information we can get, and also with care. There is nothing— one mistake can make this whole thing blow up. So that, one major mistake either by Mr. Khrushchev or by us here—so that is why it is much easier to make speeches about some of the things which we ought to be doing, but I think that anybody who looks at the fatality lists on atomic weapons, and realizes that the Communists have a completely twisted view of the United States, and that we don't comprehend them, that is what makes life in the sixties hazardous.

MR. HERMAN: Your discussion of contact with the Soviet Union, of operating and acting with care, leads me irresistibly to the picture of Mr. Gromyko sitting right here, perhaps on this very couch—

THE PRESIDENT: Right here.

MR. HERMAN: Right there—just before—

THE PRESIDENT: Right next to Mr. Vanocur.

MR. VANOCUR: He is no friend of mine.

MR. HERMAN: But there was an occasion when you were in contact. He spoke to you. He told you his very interesting version of the absence of all missiles in Cuba, of the absence of all offensive missiles in Cuba. Now, you were in contact. What did you have to do? Did you have to get up and grit your teeth and walk around the chair?

THE PRESIDENT: No, I read to him my September statement, in which we said we would take action if they put missiles in. He did not respond. That is why I say, we are quite a long way from being—Mr. Khrushchev and I are in the same boat in the sense of both having this nuclear capacity, and also both wanting to protect our societies. Where we are not on the same wave is that the Soviets expand their power and are determined to, and have demonstrated in Cuba their willingness to take great risks, which can only bring about a direct collision. Now, I spent a whole day at Vienna talking about his speech he made on January 6, 1961, in which he said he was going to support wars of liberation, and I said this is the way for the United States and the Soviet Union to end up in direct confrontation, which is what happened in Cuba. You can't have too many of those, because we are not sure on every occasion that the Soviet Union will withdraw as they did in the case of Cuba. And the United States finds it difficult to withdraw when our vital interests are involved.

MR. LAWRENCE: Mr. President, were you tempted at any time when Gromyko sat there open-faced and said that there were no offensive weapons, to just get up and go to your desk and pick up a photograph—

THE PRESIDENT: No, because our information was incomplete and we had not completely determined what our policy would be. The information came in Tuesday, our conversation was on Thursday. We were carrying out intensive reconnaissance. We were still considering the advisability of another course of action. And therefore, it would have been very unwise for us to inform him in detail what we knew. We did not want to give him the satisfaction of announcing what he was doing. I think it was very important that the United States announced it before he did.

MR. LAWRENCE: We might have lost the initiative then?

THE PRESIDENT: Yes. He might have announced it, and we would have been responding then to an initiative of theirs. This way we held the initiative. So it was very important that we not tell him, although I did not mislead him, because as I say, I read my September statement, and he must have wondered why I was reading it. But he did not respond.

MR. VANOCUR: Mr. President, a lot of people have said that it is necessary—and these are a lot of the Kremlinologists who have some knowledge about the Soviet Union—that it is necessary for an American President to protect Mr. Khrushchev, because he is the best Soviet prime minister we will ever get. Do you feel that is really the duty of an American President or it is the duty of an American President to protect the national interest?

THE PRESIDENT: No, I don't think it is our duty to protect Mr. Khrushchev. This argument that his successor would be worse—I don't know what his successor will be like. What I think is our duty is to try to protect our vital interests, protect the security of the free world, and have Mr. Khrushchev understand our intentions clearly enough so that he can proceed about his business in a way which does not threaten our security, and does not bring a war. We don't want to have to protect our security by means of war. But Mr. Khrushchev has to understand that there are vital interests in the United States for which we will fight, and if he will come—he and the Communists and the Soviet Union will come to devote their energies to demonstrating how their system works in the Soviet Union, it seems to me his vital interests are easily protected with the power that he has, and we could have a long period of peace. Then we could make a judgment which system does do the job. We believe ours does. He has argued that his does, internally. But instead, by these constant desires to change the balance of power in the world, that is what, it seems to me, introduces the dangerous element.

Now, I do think in fairness, if you read his speech this week, you can see that we would be far worse off—the world would be —if the Chinese dominated the Communist movement, because they believe in war as the means of bringing about the Communist world. Mr. Khrushchev's means are destruction, but he believes that peaceful coexistence and support of these wars of liberation, small wars, will bring about our defeat. The Chinese Communists believe that by constantly hitting, and if war comes, a nuclear third world war, they can survive it anyway with 750 million people. So we are better off with the Khrushchev view than we are with the Chinese Communist view, quite obviously. But Mr. Khrushchev does not wish us well, unfortunately.

MR. VANOCUR: Is there anything we can do to influence this growing split within the Communist bloc, or should we just tend to the world that we have, and make sure that it is not ripe for Communist penetration?

THE PRESIDENT: I think that this dispute which has become intensified is a matter that—I think if we would, as you suggest, devote our attention to so much of the world which is in very desperate condition, some of the countries of Latin America, Africa, Asia, which need our assistance, which need our support, if we do our job of strengthening the free world, then we will be, it seems to me, creating pressure, a counterpressure against the Communist advance, and that communism internally, under that kind of pressure, will find its lot more difficult.

I do think we have a tendency to think of the world as Communist and free, as if it were two units. The fact of the matter is our world is so divided, so poverty-stricken, so desperate in many conditions, that we have a full-time job just strengthening the section of the world which is not Communist, all of Africa, newly independent and poverty-stricken. Here we have the prime minister of Somali who came the other day—$45 per year the per capita income. The average wage in the United States manufacture is about $94 a week. Forty-five dollars a year! Well, now, he has got staggering problems. You can go through Latin America and parts of northeast Brazil—$100 a year they are living on. So we have got a big job to do in our own area. If we can strengthen that area, as communism in my opinion is a completely fallacious—and really is a system which really does not suit the desires of the average man—then I think we can be successful.

MR. HERMAN: During the Cuban crisis when there was an offer of inspection inside Cuba by Premier Khrushchev, did you have any hope that there might be a breakthrough, a start to achieving some kind of peace between our two systems, so that we can work on our own problems?

THE PRESIDENT: No, I don't think that is there yet. Now, it may come in time.

MR. HERMAN: Did you have hope when it was offered that it might actually come about?

THE PRESIDENT: No, but I do think at least that Cuba, as I think the speech this week, which was an important speech—has made Mr. Khrushchev aware of the dangers of the United States and the Soviet Union clashing over an area of vital importance. So that I think is a very salutary fact. But I don't think we are about to see a whole change in Communist policy.

MR. HERMAN: Would there have been any breakthrough if there had been international inspection of Cuba allowed, do you think, a start, a thin edge of a wedge?

THE PRESIDENT: No, I don't think that would have materially affected it, because I don't think we would have gotten the kind of inspection which really is necessary, because a totalitarian system cannot accept the kind of inspection which really is desirable. What you are really saying is that Cuba be opened, the Soviet Union be opened. They are not going to open it, because a totalitarian system must exist only in secrecy.

MR. HERMAN: Have the inspections that we have had anywhere in the world, for example, in North Korea, or anyplace else, given you any hope that it will work as a system?

THE PRESIDENT: No, the camera, I think, is actually going to be our best inspector.

MR. LAWRENCE: Mr. President, is there anything in the end of the Cuban crisis or the substantial end of it, at least getting off a fever pitch, and other problems around the world that would lead you to think that a summit meeting would be useful any time in the near future?

THE PRESIDENT: No, not just now. I think that the Vienna meeting was useful. It was useful for me, and I think—but I don't think we should go back to that, unless we really see our way clear to making an agreement on nuclear testing or disarmament, or in Europe itself, coming to some understanding. That is what we really want to do. As I say, this is too dangerous a period for us to be or to want to have a tension between the Soviet Union and the United States, and therefore I think we should encourage any relaxation of their policy of supporting those causes hostile to us. But until we see some breakthrough in some one area, I don't see there is much advantage in Mr. Khrushchev and I meeting, even though we have been in communication, and therefore I think at least we have some—and we are in negotiation in New York through our representatives, but

I don't think there is a need for us to meet now. I think probably he feels the same way.

MR. LAWRENCE: Many expected, Mr. President, that Berlin would "hot up" right after our elections. That seemed to be the timetable, perhaps incorrectly. Is there any feeling on your part that what happened in Cuba has led to greater caution in Berlin insofar as the Soviet and East German governments are concerned?

THE PRESIDENT: Oh, I think the chairman—nobody wants to go through what we went through in Cuba very often, and I think they realize that West Berlin is a vital interest to us, and that we are committed there, and that we are going to stay there. On the other hand, he has a very vital interest in East Germany, in trying to prop up that regime, and trying to solidify his position in Eastern Europe. So Berlin is a dangerous position always, particularly because of its geography, because we have to keep communications to an area which is 120 miles behind their lines. So this always gives them a chance to tighten the grip on our windpipe there. But I would think he would proceed with some care, because I think he realizes it is the combination of a vital interest and one which has the chance of a direct encounter. So that I think that, as I say, Mr. Khrushchev's speech showed that he knows. And those who are attacking Mr. Khrushchev in the Communist camp, particularly the Chinese, as being too soft— I think Mr. Khrushchev realizes the care with which he must proceed now, as do we.

MR. HERMAN: Would you explain, sir, why you said in your toast to Chancellor Adenauer that this was a turning point, a new era in history.

THE PRESIDENT: I think it is a climactic period. We have had a number of them. It is not *the*, but it is. After all, Cuba was the first time that the Soviet Union and the United States directly faced each other with the prospect of the use of military forces being used by the United States and the Soviet Union, which could possibly have escalated into a nuclear struggle. That is an important fact. Secondly, the Chinese-Indian struggle—between these two enormous countries, the two largest countries in the world—when the Soviet has devoted so many years to building its policy of friendship with India, the fact that China then attacked them. And third, the relation between the Soviet Union and China, as a result of the Sino-Indian dispute, as a result of the United States dispute with the Soviet Union over Cuba, I would say that that makes this a very important period.

MR. VANOCUR: How do you as the leader of the Western alliance, of the strongest member nation—how do you get the European countries, which are becoming increasingly more independent, increasingly more prosperous, which is what you said you hoped they would become—how do you get them to follow your lead? Apparently Secretaries McNamara and Rusk have not come back with an altogether satisfactory report from the NATO meeting; the Europeans seem unwilling to build conventional forces. Do you have any great power to determine—

THE PRESIDENT: No, in the first place you can do your part. We are doing our part. We have—our troops in Western Europe are the best equipped. We have six divisions, which is about a fourth of all of the divisions on the Western front. They are the best equipped. They can fight tomorrow, which is not true of most of the other units. So we are doing our part there, and we are also providing the largest naval force in the world. We are also providing the nuclear force in the world, and we are also carrying out the major space program for the free world, as well as carrying the whole burden in South Vietnam. So the United States is more than doing its part. We hope Western Europe will make a greater effort on its own, both in developing conventional forces, and in assistance to the underdeveloped world.

Now, we can't force them to do it. We can't say, "Well, if you won't do it, we are going to withdraw our forces and leave Europe naked." But I think the United States has done pretty well in carrying its burdens, and we hope that Western Europe, now that it is prosperous, will do its part. We put $12 billion in Western Europe in four years, from 1948 to 1952. The amount of assistance we have given Latin American for the Alliance for Progress is a fraction of that.

So we have a right, it seems to me, as we have done and proven that we are not sunshine soldiers with respect to Europe itself. There isn't a country in Europe that is putting—of the countries that we are talking about—that is putting as many men and as large a proportion of its population and its gross national product into defense as we are.

MR. VANOCUR: Well, sir, do you reach a point where you have to say, "Fish or cut bait; I can't go to the American people and ask them to assume this burden if they know that you are going to do this?" For example, the Skybolt.

THE PRESIDENT: Well, look at the Skybolt. The United States has developed the Skybolt. We put in $350 million into Skybolt. No other country has put anything into the actual manufacture of Skybolt. If we completed it, the British would have bought a hundred missiles, we would have bought a thousand. It would have cost us $2.5 billion. We today pay 30 per cent of the infrastructure costs of NATO, the supply lines to the depots in Europe. It costs us about $3 billion in our balance of payments. The aid we give around the world is—you know, the American people are very critical, and the American press prints a lot of bad news, because bad news is news and good news is not news, so they get an impression always that the United States is not doing its part. When I just think of what we have done for fifteen years, since 1945—the countries we have sustained; the alliances of which we are the whole, the center; the willingness of the United States to accept burdens all around the world—I think it is a fantastic story. We have one million Americans today serving outside the United States. There is no other country in history that has carried this kind of a burden. The other countries who had forces serving outside of their own country but for conquest. We have two divisions in South Korea, not to control South Korea, but to defend it. We have a lot of Americans in South Vietnam. Well, now, no other country in the world has ever done that since the beginning of the world; Greece, Rome, Napoleon, and all the rest, always had conquest. We have a million men outside and they are trying to defend these countries. Now what we are saying is that rich Western Europe must do its part, and I hope it will.

MR. HERMAN: Nothing that a President ever says is without effect, Mr. Kennedy. Aren't you sure that these words that you have just uttered will come back to you when the appropriations bill starts through the Congress, that you will hear yourself quoted?

THE PRESIDENT: No, I think the American people ought to know what they are doing, and I think Western Europe—Western Europe's success, after all, represents the greatest success of American foreign policy, since World War II, the rebuilding of Europe. It is just what we want. They are bound to have differences of opinion with us. But all we ask Western Europe to do is not look in and just become a rich, careful, secluded group, but to play their role in this great world struggle, as we have done it. We are going to continue to do it in the United States, but we ought to recognize how much we have done, and not always be feeling—whenever I read a dispatch from Europe, it is usually rather critical, even in the Skybolt stories that come out are critical of the United States. My goodness, we have done a tremendous job in this country.

MR. HERMAN: But can they play their role without developing their own nuclear weapons and their own nuclear deterrent, and isn't it against our policy to have this proliferation?

THE PRESIDENT: Well, we don't want six or seven nuclear powers in Europe diverting their funds to nuclear power, when the United States has got this tremendous arsenal. But if these countries want to do it, we are not stopping them from doing it. If the French decide they want to become a nuclear power themselves, that is their decision. The question is whether the United States should join in helping make France a nuclear power, then Italy, then West Germany, then Belgium. How does that produce security when you have ten, twenty, thirty nuclear powers who may fire their weapons off under different conditions? That isn't in our interest, or in my opinion in the interest of peace, or the interest of Western Europe. And it is awfully expensive. Why duplicate what we have already done, and are doing in Western Europe today, as long as our guarantees are good?

MR. VANOCUR: Mr. President, back before you were elected, your father used to have a favorite story he told reporters. He asked you once why do you want the job, and he cited the reasons why you shouldn't want it, and you apparently gave him an answer. I don't know whether it satisfied him, but apparently you satisfied yourself. Would you give him the same answer today after serving in this office for two years?

THE PRESIDENT: Oh, you mean that somebody is going to do it?

MR. VANOCUR: Yes, sir.

THE PRESIDENT: Yes. I think that there are a lot of satisfactions to the presidency, particularly, as I say, we are all concerned as citizens and as parents and all the rest, with all the problems we have been talking about tonight. They are all the problems which if I was not the President, I would be concerned about as a father or as a citizen. So at least you have an opportunity to do something about them. And if what you do is useful and successful, then of course that is a great satisfaction. When as a result of a decision of yours, failure comes, or you are unsuccessful, then of course that is a great setback. But I must say after being here for two years, and having the experience of the presidency—and there is no experience you can get that can possibly prepare you adequately for the presidency—I must say that I have a good deal of hope for the United States. Just because I think that this country, which as I say criticizes itself and is criticized around the world, 180 million people, for seventeen years—really for more than that, for almost twenty years—have been the great means of defending first the world against the Nazi threat, and since then against the Communist threat, and if it were not for us, the Communists would be dominant in the world today, and because of us, we are in a strong position. Now, I think that is a pretty good record for a country with 6 per cent of the world's population, which is very reluctant to take on these burdens. I think we ought to be rather pleased with ourselves this Christmas.

INTRODUCTION AND FAREWELL

INAUGURAL ADDRESS [1]

WILLIAM W. SCRANTON [2]

Last November, William W. Scranton was elected governor of Pennsylvania by a substantial margin over his Democratic opponent, Richardson Dilworth. Through his victory, he became a possible contender—along with Nelson A. Rockefeller, Barry Goldwater, and George Romney—for the Republican presidential nomination in 1964. Young, personable, and highly articulate, Mr. Scranton moved to the top state office after serving only a two-year apprenticeship in politics as a member of the Eighty-seventh Congress from the Tenth District of Pennsylvania. He campaigned vigorously on the economic issues affecting the state of Pennsylvania.

On January 15, 1963, Mr. Scranton took the oath of office as the forty-first constitutional governor of the Commonwealth and the one hundred and third since colonial times. Some 13,000 persons attended the ceremony at the State Farm Show building arena in Harrisburg where the governor delivered a short inaugural address over a state-wide television network. The message was largely a call for unity. In simple, inspirational expression—virtually free from partisan overtones—he urged Pennsylvanians to dedicate their strength and resources to putting the state on the march "toward greatness for herself" and "progress for her people."

Within a week after his inauguration, Mr. Scranton had outlined an ambitious legislative program calling for the creation of new agencies to deal with community and health programs, expansion of civil service, increases in medical aid under the Kerr-Mills Act, and a referendum for revision of the state constitution. Said Frederick W. Roevekamp, staff correspondent of the *Christian Science Monitor*:

> If the new Pennsylvania governor, a strikingly successful newcomer to politics, manages to put most of his program through the more conservative Republican state legislature, his national political stature is also likely to continue its rapid rise.

[1] Text furnished by William Keisling, assistant to Governor Scranton, with permission for this reprint.

[2] For biographical note, see Appendix.

Some observers feel, however, that "there is something politically fatal" about a stint in the capitol at Harrisburg. Joseph A. Loftus, writing in the New York *Times*, said "the four-year term is a rocky road to unpopularity." And he quotes Mr. Scranton as saying, "If I were going to run for President I wouldn't have run for governor."

My fellow Pennsylvanians:

Nearly three hundred years ago a God-fearing man carved the first bits of civilization out of the land that lay west of the Delaware.

His name was William Penn. He had an idea. It took root in our soil.

His idea was that men and women are resourceful and imaginative.

He believed that, given a chance, they could turn back a wilderness, chisel out a monument to human dignity, and live in peace and prosperity.

In an age rife with human hatred, with religious bigotry, with political persecution, he had the wisdom, and the courage, to launch a Holy Experiment.

He made Pennsylvania the bastion of freedom, the temple of tolerance, the showcase of economic enterprise.

He believed freedom is more than a cliché. He believed courage is more than a slogan. He believed human will power more than a match for all the obstacles of nature or economics. He believed human ingenuity capable of solving human problems. He believed indifference and despair can be put to rout by human hope.

But, most of all he believed in himself, he believed in his fellow men, he believed in Pennsylvania.

That was three centuries ago.

Three months ago I was campaigning through a Pennsylvania town. The day was dreary. A cold rain had drizzled down all morning.

A young man with tired eyes, a sad voice and a scared handshake told me: "Pennsylvania is no place for me."

And, a day later, I campaigned through a sun-drenched suburb. Other people with other, quite different, problems.

Another young man, this one with a kind of "I'm going places" look about him grasped my hand. He looked me in the eye. He said: "I can't for the life of me figure out why any-body would want to be governor of this state."

And he explained, "Pennsylvania is going nowhere."

That was three months ago.

Three days ago I pondered what to say on the day that I became governor of this state.

I thought of William Penn three hundred years ago. But I remembered the young man of three months ago.

With this memory the vim and vigor of the campaign seemed to sour. The flush of election victory paled. The brave hopes of just yesterday seemed puny. The awful responsibility seemed to dwarf the high honor of the office I was about to assume.

But then more of Pennsylvania came to mind. More of what we have been taught and know of Pennsylvania. More of her heritage. More of her people, and their pride and their faith, the hands I had clasped, the warmth of their welcome.

I remembered the face of the woman. Woman of a town blasted by industrial migration. Plants closed. Gates locked. Menfolk idle. I remembered the courage in the face of the woman.

I remembered the eyes of the man. Man out of work. Tiny worry lines around those eyes. The haunting fear that self-respect might flee, but even stronger, the challenge: "Give me a chance, and you'll see what I can do." I remembered the hope in the eyes of the man.

I remembered the hands of the farmer. A sower of seeds. A cultivator of life. A man close to God. Hands flecked with soil, so the tan of the skin seemed almost one with the tan of the earth. Hands that make things grow. I remembered the pride of those hands.

I remembered the arms that swung a lunch pail. Skilled arms. Strong sinews. A cadence to his walk that said: "I do a day's work. I do it well." Perhaps the proudest boast of man. I remembered the fresh, pungent smell of independence.

I remembered the frown of the young college student. In-quisitive. Prove it or I won't believe it. Why can't Pennsyl-vania move ahead? Who says my only opportunities lie else-where? Is it wrong to care? What are you going to do about it? Yes, I remembered the anxious student.

And, I remembered the brow of a businessman. Furrowed? Yes, but perhaps even more accurately, concerned. "I have a duty here. A role to perform. I want Pennsylvania to climb to the top. I'm busy and it's easy to find excuses, but point the way and I'll do my share." Yes, I remember the concern, the willingness, in that face.

And, suddenly, I knew that Pennsylvania today is not really very different than the Pennsylvania of three centuries ago.

Yes, the challenges wear different faces. Problems assume different guises. But truly, we hold the same trump cards.

Resourcefulness, imagination, fortitude. And one more—faith.

The Pennsylvania that responded to the seventeenth century promise of William Penn's Holy Experiment;

The Pennsylvania that nurtured an eighteenth century Ben Franklin and became the cradle of liberty;

The Pennsylvania that was strengthened by a nineteenth century influx of brave, stout hearts from the Old World;

The Pennsylvania that in the twentieth century has remained basically strong and vital, despite a buffeting from history's greatest technological revolution;

That Pennsylvania—don't tell me that Pennsylvania can't lick its problems, because I know it can.

We still have the same God-given natural resources, the same advantages for commerce and industry, the same progressive spirit that brought us greatness in other years, in other ages.

But, these things must be tapped. Resources and advantages and spirit must be put to work. Human courage and human hope must drive the motors of human effort and human toil.

Some of Pennsylvania's problems can be solved soon; others can only be solved in time. But nothing will happen, nothing will move, unless the labor begins today.

The state government has an obvious and vital role in that labor. As a Pennsylvanian, no one can convince me that our state is incapable of that labor. No one can convince me that other states and other governments are more capable.

Of course, there are those who would prefer to dwell more on our fears than on our hopes.

There are those who would prefer to curse the darkness, rather than light a candle. Blame the past, rather than work to assure the future.

There are those who would prefer to gossip of yesterday's divisions, rather than work on today's need for unity.

Show me a Democrat who was wrong or shortsighted; I will show you a Republican who was. And vice-versa.

Show me a businessman who was selfish; I will show you a labor leader who was. And vice-versa.

Show me a citizen in Pennsylvania who has suffered by someone's lack of concern, and I will show you another citizen who has caused suffering by his lack of concern.

But let us hope that in the showing, both you and I will grow wiser and learn that today's opportunities are far more important than yesterday's mistakes.

With these opportunities, Pennsylvania is on the march. Toward greatness for herself. Toward progress, for her people.

Our Commonwealth has the resources, the human strength, the get-up-and-go from which greatness is made. There is work to do, lots of it, but Pennsylvanians have never shirked from that prospect.

In both the executive branch and in the legislature, all of us must vow today to do our part to bring about a new era in Pennsylvania progress. We must have the wisdom to keep what should be kept; the courage to change what should be changed.

With the help of God let us embrace the challenge, let us welcome the labor.

Let us stand tall as Pennsylvanians.

Let us walk proudly as Pennsylvanians.

EULOGY ON ELEANOR ROOSEVELT [3]

Adlai E. Stevenson [4]

Mrs. Franklin D. Roosevelt died November 7, 1962. Three days later she was buried next to her husband on the family estate at Hyde Park, New York. At the funeral, the Reverend Dr. Gordon L. Kidd, rector of St. James's Protestant Episcopal Church, departed momentarily from the Book of Common Prayer liturgy to recite Mrs. Roosevelt's favorite prayer:

> Lord, make me an instrument of your peace.
> Where there is hatred, let me sow love,
> Where there is injury, pardon,
> Where there is doubt, faith,
> Where there is despair, hope,
> Where there is darkness, light,
> Where there is sadness, joy.
>
> O Divine Master, grant that I may seek
>   not so much to be consoled as to console,
>
> To be understood as to understand,
> To be loved as to love,
> For it is in giving that we receive,
> It is in pardoning that we are pardoned,
> And it is in dying that we are born to eternal life.

Mrs. Roosevelt's life richly embodied the substance of the Prayer of St. Francis of Assisi. She was, as Max Ascoli wrote soon after her death, "utterly selfless, and what she gave to the world in her indiscriminate wholeheartedness will bear fruit for a long, long time."

At a memorial service on November 17 at the Cathedral of St. John the Divine in New York City, some ten thousand persons heard a moving eulogy on Mrs. Roosevelt delivered by her close friend Ambassador Adlai E. Stevenson, United States representative to the United Nations. The service was attended by dignitaries from at home and abroad, and by men and women of all ages and races and economic station. Not a seat in the large cathedral was unoccupied; many persons stood in the aisles, as Mr. Stevenson spoke with quiet eloquence of the remembrance which now begins.

---

[3] Text furnished by Mr. Stevenson, with permission for this reprint. The lines by Archibald MacLeish are reprinted by his permission.

[4] For biographical note, see Appendix.

One week ago this afternoon, in the Rose Garden at Hyde Park, Eleanor Roosevelt came home for the last time. Her journeys are over. The remembrance now begins.

In gathering here to honor her, we engage in a self-serving act. It is we who are trying, by this ceremony of tribute, to deny the fact that we have lost her, and, at least, to prolong the farewell, and—possibly—to say some of the things we dared not say in her presence, because she would have turned aside such testimonial with impatience and gently asked us to get on with some of the more serious business of the meeting.

A grief perhaps not equaled since the death of her husband seventeen years ago is the world's best tribute to one of the great figures of our age—a woman whose lucid and luminous faith testified always for sanity in an insane time and for hope in a time of obscure hope—a woman who spoke for the good toward which man aspires in a world which has seen too much of the evil of which man is capable.

She lived seventy-eight years, most of the time in tireless activity as if she knew that only a frail fragment of the things that cry out to be done could be done in the lifetime of even the most fortunate. One has the melancholy sense that when she knew death was at hand, she was contemplating not what she achieved, but what she had not quite managed to do. And I know she wanted to go—when there was no more strength to do.

Yet how much she had done—how much still unchronicled! We dare not try to tabulate the lives she salvaged, the battles—known and unrecorded—she fought, the afflicted she comforted, the hovels she brightened, the faces and places, near and far, that were given some new radiance, some sound of music, by her endeavors. What other single human being has touched and transformed the existence of so many others? What better measure is there of the impact of anyone's life?

There was no sick soul too wounded to engage her mercy. There was no signal of human distress which she did not view as a personal summons. There was no affront to human dignity from which she fled because the timid cried "danger." And the number of occasions on which her intervention turned despair into victory we may never know.

Her life was crowded, restless, fearless. Perhaps she pitied most not those whom she aided in the struggle, but the more fortunate who were preoccupied with themselves and cursed with the self-deceptions of private success. She walked in the slums and ghettos of the world, not on a tour of inspection, nor as a condescending patron, but as one who could not feel complacent while others were hungry, and who could not find contentment while others were in distress. This was not sacrifice; this, for Mrs. Roosevelt, was the only meaningful way of life.

These were not conventional missions of mercy. What rendered this unforgettable woman so extraordinary was not merely her response to suffering; it was her comprehension of the complexity of the human condition. Not long before she died, she wrote that "within all of us there are two sides. One reaches for the stars, the other descends to the level of beasts." It was, I think, this discernment that made her so unfailingly tolerant of friends who faltered, and led her so often to remind the smug and the complacent that "there but for the grace of God. . . ."

But we dare not regard her as just a benign incarnation of good works. For she was not only a great woman and a great humanitarian, but a great democrat. I use the word with a small "d"—though it was, of course, equally true that she was a great Democrat with a capital "D." When I say that she was a great small "d" democrat, I mean that she had a lively and astute understanding of the nature of the democratic process. She was a master political strategist with a fine sense of humor. And, as she said, she loved a good fight.

She was a realist. Her compassion did not become sentimentality. She understood that progress was a long labor of compromise. She mistrusted absolutism in all its forms—the absolutism of the word and even more the absolutism of the deed. She never supposed that all the problems of life could be cured in a day or a year or a lifetime. Her pungent and salty understanding of human behavior kept her always in intimate contact with reality. I think this was a primary source of her strength, because she never thought that the loss of a battle meant the loss of a war, nor did she suppose that a compromise which produced only part of the objective sought was an act of corruption or of treachery. She knew that no formula of words, no combination of deeds, could abolish the troubles of life overnight and usher in the millennium.

The miracle, I have tried to suggest, is how much tangible good she really did; how much realism and reason were mingled with her instinctive compassion; how her contempt for the perquisites of power ultimately won her the esteem of so many of the powerful; and how, at her death, there was a universality of grief that transcended all the harsh boundaries of political, racial and religious strife and, for a moment at least, united men in a vision of what their world might be.

We do not claim the right to enshrine another mortal, and this least of all would Mrs. Roosevelt have desired. She would have wanted it said, I believe, that she well knew the pressures of pride and vanity, the sting of bitterness and defeat, the gray days of national peril and personal anguish. But she clung to the confident expectation that men could fashion their own tomorrows if they could only learn that yesterday can be neither relived nor revised.

Many who have spoken of her in these last few days have used a word to which we all assent, because it speaks a part of what we feel. They have called her "a lady," a "great lady," "the first lady of the world." But the word "lady," though it says much about Eleanor Roosevelt, does not say all. To be incapable of self-concern is not a negative virtue; it is the other side of a coin that has a positive face—the most positive, I think, of all the faces. And to enhance the humanity of others is not a kind of humility; it is a kind of pride—the noblest of all the forms of pride. No man or woman can respect other men and women who does not respect life. And to respect life is to love it. Eleanor Roosevelt loved life—and that, perhaps, is the most meaningful thing that can be said about her, for it says so much beside.

It takes courage to love life. Loving it demands imagination and perception and the kind of patience women are more apt to have than men—the bravest and most understanding women. And loving it takes something more beside—it takes a gift for life, a gift for love.

Eleanor Roosevelt's childhood was unhappy—miserably unhappy, she sometimes said. But it was Eleanor Roosevelt who also said that "one must never, for whatever reason, turn his back on life." She did not mean that duty should compel us. She meant that life should. "Life," she said, "was meant to be lived." A simple statement. An obvious statement. But a statement that by its obviousness and its simplicity challenges the most intricate of all the philosophies of despair.

Many of the admonitions she bequeathed us are neither new thoughts nor novel concepts. Her ideas were, in many respects, old-fashioned—as old as the Sermon on the Mount, as the reminder that it is more blessed to give than to receive. In the words of St. Francis that she loved so well: "For it is in the giving that we receive."

She imparted to the familiar language—nay, what too many have come to treat as the clichés—of Christianity a new poignancy and vibrance. She did so not by reciting them, but by proving that it is possible to live them. It is this above all that rendered her unique in her century. It was said of her contemptuously at times that she was a do-gooder, a charge leveled with similar derision against another public figure 1,962 years ago.

We who are assembled here are of various religious and political faiths, and perhaps different conceptions of man's destiny in the universe. It is not an irreverence, I trust, to say that the immortality Mrs. Roosevelt would have valued most would be found in the deeds and visions her life inspired in others, and in the proof that they would be faithful to the spirit of any tribute conducted in her name.

And now one can almost hear Mrs. Roosevelt saying that the speaker has already talked too long. So we must say farewell. We are always saying farewell in this world—always standing at the edge of loss attempting to retrieve some memory, some human meaning, from the silence—something which was precious and is gone.

Often, although we know the absence well enough, we cannot name it or describe it even. What left the world when Lincoln died? Speaker after speaker in those aching days tried to tell his family or his neighbors or his congregation. But no one found the words, not even Whitman. "When lilacs last in the dooryard bloomed" can break the heart, but not with Lincoln's greatness, only with his loss. What the words could never capture was the man himself. His deeds were known; every school child knew them. But it was not his deeds the country mourned: it was the man—the mastery of life which made the greatness of the man.

It is always so. On that April day when Franklin Roosevelt died, it was not a President we wept for. It was a man. In Archibald MacLeish's words:

Fagged out, worn down, sick
With the weight of his own bones,
                    the task finished,
The war won, the victory assured,
The glory left behind him for
                    the others,
(And the wheels roll up through
        the night in the sweet land
In the cool air in the spring
        between the lanterns).

It is so now. What we have lost in Eleanor Roosevelt is not her life. She lived that out to the full. What we have lost, what we wish to recall for ourselves, to remember, is what she was herself. And who can name it? But she left "a name to shine on the entablatures of truth, forever."

We pray that she has found peace, and a glimpse of sunset. But today we weep for ourselves. We are lonelier; someone has gone from one's own life—who was like the certainty of refuge; and someone has gone from the world—who was like a certainty of honor.

APPENDIX

BIOGRAPHICAL NOTES

COMMONER, BARRY (1917-   ). Born, Brooklyn, New York; A.B., Columbia University, 1937; Ph.D., Harvard University, 1941; assistant in biology, Harvard University, 1938-40; instructor, Queens College, 1940-42; lieutenant, United States Naval Reserve, active duty 1942-46 (naval liaison officer, United States Senate Committee on Military Affairs, subcommittee on war mobilization to assist in preparation of National Science Foundation bill, 1946); associate professor of plant physiology, Washington University, 1947-53; professor, 1953-   ; chairman, committee on molecular biology, Washington University, 1957-61; secretary, committee on cancer research, 1953-58; chairman, planning council for biology, 1962-   ; chairman, committee on science in the promotion of human welfare, American Association for the Advancement of Science, 1958; chairman, botanical section, 1960-61; chairman, committee on research grants, 1954-60; member, committee on council activities, 1960-   ; vice president, St. Louis committee for nuclear information, 1958-   ; member, American Institute of Biological Sciences long-range planning council, 1961-   ; member, honorary advisory panel, *Problems of Virology*, 1957-   ; council member, Federation of American Scientists, 1957; Society of General Physiologists, 1961; chapter president, Washington University, Society of Sigma Xi, 1957-58; chapter president, American Association of University Professors, 1958; member, board of directors and executive committee, Scientists Institute for Public Information, 1963-   ; associate editor, *Science Illustrated*, 1946-47; member of editorial board, *International Review of Cytology*, 1957-   ; *American Naturalist*, 1959-   ; *Theoretical Biology*, 1960-   ; recipient, Newcomb Cleveland prize, American Association for the Advancement of Science, 1953; Phi Beta Kappa; Sigma Xi.

EISELEY, LOREN (1907-   ). Born, Lincoln, Nebraska; A.B., University of Nebraska, 1933; A.M., University of Pennsylvania, 1935; Ph.D., 1937; postdoctoral work at Columbia University and the American Museum of Natural History; honorary degrees from New York University, Western Reserve University, University of Nebraska, and Franklin and Marshall College; assistant professor, sociology and anthropology, University of Kansas, 1937-42; associate professor, 1942-44; head, department of sociology and anthropology, Oberlin College, 1944-47; professor and head of department of anthropology, University of Pennsylvania, 1947-59; provost, 1959-61; professor of anthropology and chairman of department of history and philosophy of science, 1961- ; curator of Museum of Early Man, University of Pennsylvania, 1948- ; president, American Institute of Human Paleontology, 1949-52; fellow, American Association for the Advancement of Science; member, National Research Council; president, Philadelphia Anthropological Society, 1948; member, American Philosophical Society; recipient, Page One Award, Newspaper Guild, Pennsylvania, 1960; Phi Beta Kappa; Sigma Xi; co-editor, *An Appraisal of Anthropology Today*, 1953; author, *The Immense Journey*, 1957; *Darwin's Century: Evolution and the Men Who Discovered It*, 1958; *The Firmament of Time*, 1960; *Francis Bacon and the Modern Dilemma*, 1960; *The Mind as Nature*, 1962; contributor to journals and periodicals.

FISCHER, JOHN H. (1910-). Born, Baltimore, Maryland; received diploma, Maryland State Teachers College, 1930; B.S., Johns Hopkins University, 1940; M.A., Teachers College, Columbia University, 1949; Ed.D., 1951; honorary degrees, Morgan State College, 1955, Goucher College, 1959; associated with Baltimore public school system, 1930-59: teacher, 1930-35; vice principal, 1935-38; special assistant at Benjamin Franklin junior high school, 1938-42; director of school attendance and child guidance in Baltimore system, 1942-45; assistant superintendent for general administration, 1945-52; deputy superintendent of schools, 1952-53; superintendent of public instruction, 1953-59; dean, Teachers College, Columbia University, 1959-62; president, 1962- ; president, Maryland State Teachers Association, 1945; president, Baltimore Council of Social Agencies, 1957-59; member, National Education Association; national advisory council

of United States Peace Corps; American Association of School
Administrators; author, journal and periodical articles. (See also
Current Biography: 1960.)

GOULD, SAMUEL B. (1910-   ). Born, New York City; A.B.,
Bates College, 1930; A.M., New York University, 1936; attended
Oxford University, 1931; Cambridge University, 1934; Harvard
University, 1941; LL.D., Bates College, 1957; LL.D., Wilberforce
University, 1960; assignment on radio staff, Providence, Rhode
Island, 1931; Hartford, Connecticut, 1938; instructor, William
Hall high school, West Hartford, Connecticut, 1932-38; head of
speech department, Brookline, Massachusetts, schools, 1938-47;
director of communications division, Boston University, 1947-50;
assistant to president, 1950-53; associated with management engineers firm, 1953; president, Antioch College, 1954-59; chancellor, University of California at Santa Barbara, 1959-62; president,
Educational Broadcasting Corporation, New York City, 1962- ;
director, American Labor Education Service; lieutenant commander, United States Naval Reserve, World War II; awarded
Commendation Ribbon, Presidential Unit Citation with bronze
star; trustee, Wilberforce University; Thomas Alva Edison
Foundation; Educational Records Bureau; member, English
Speaking Union; Phi Beta Kappa; Delta Sigma Rho; author,
Training the Local Announcer, 1950; co-author, *Knowledge Is
Not Enough*, 1959. (See also *Current Biography: 1958.*)

HESBURGH, THEODORE M. (1917-   ). Born, Syracuse, New
York; graduate, Holy Rosary high school, 1934; student, University of Notre Dame, 1934-37; Ph.B., Gregorian University, Rome,
Italy, 1940; advanced work in theology, Holy Cross College,
Washington, 1940-43; S.T.D., Catholic University of America,
1945; honorary degrees from LeMoyne College; University of
Santiago, Chile; Dartmouth College; Bradley University; Villa-
nova University; and other institutions; entered Order of Congregation of the Holy Cross, 1934; ordained priest, University
of Notre Dame, 1943; auxiliary chaplain, United States Army,
World War II; veterans' chaplain, University of Notre Dame,
1945-47; head, department of religion, University of Notre Dame,

1948-49; executive vice president, 1949-52; president, 1952- ; member, United States Civil Rights Commission, 1957- ; member, National Science Board; Institute of International Education; American Council on Education; Association of American Colleges; National Catholic Education Association; author, *Theology of Catholic Action*, 1945; *God and the World of Man*, 1950. (See also *Current Biography: 1955*.)

HORN, FRANCIS HENRY (1908-). Born, Toledo, Ohio; A.B., Dartmouth College, 1930; A.M., University of Virginia, 1934; Ph.D., Yale University, 1942; LL.D., University of Hartford, 1955; Providence College, 1959; D.H.L., Southern Illinois University, 1958; instructor of English and history, American University at Cairo, 1930-33; dean, Quinnipiac College, 1938-42; vice president, 1947; assistant dean, Biarritz American University in France, 1945-46; associate professor of education, Johns Hopkins University, 1947-51; president, Pratt Institute, 1953-57; president, University of Rhode Island, 1958- ; Legion of Merit, Army Commendation Medal; editor, *College and University Bulletin*, 1951-53; *Current Issues in Higher Education*, 1952; *Literary Masterpieces of the Western World*, 1953; *Twenty-Five Years in the Wide, Wide World*, 1955; contributor to magazines and journals.

KENNEDY, JOHN FITZGERALD (1917-). Born, Brookline, Massachusetts; student, London School of Economics, 1935-36; B.S., *cum laude*, Harvard University, 1940; LL.D., University of Notre Dame, 1950; Tufts College, 1954; Harvard University, 1956; served in United States Navy, 1941-45; awarded Purple Heart and other military decorations; correspondent, San Francisco United Nations Conference, British election, Potsdam meeting, 1945; United States House of Representatives (Democrat, Massachusetts), 1947-53; United States Senate, 1953-60; elected President of the United States, 1960; author, *Why England Slept*, 1940; *Profiles in Courage*, 1956 (Pulitzer prize for biography); *The Strategy of Peace*, 1960. (See also *Current Biography: 1961*.)

NORSTAD, LAURIS (1907-   ). Born, Minneapolis, Minnesota; B.S., United States Military Academy, 1930; graduate, Air Corps School, 1931; Air Corps Tactical School, Maxwell Field, Alabama, 1939; promoted through military grades to general in 1952; with General Headquarters, Air Force, 1940-42; 12th Air Force, 1943; director, plans and operation division, War Department, General Staff, 1946; acting vice chief of staff for operations, Air Forces, 1947-50; commander in chief, United States and Allied Air Forces in Central Europe, 1951; air deputy, SHAPE, 1953-56; supreme commander of military forces of NATO, 1956-62; director, Owens-Corning Fiberglas Corporation and president, Owens-Corning Fiberglas International, 1963-   ; recipient of many decorations: Distinguished Service Medal, Silver Star, Legion of Merit, Air Medal, Croix de Guerre, and others. (See also *Current Biography: 1959.*)

ROCKEFELLER, NELSON A. (1908-   ). Born, Bar Harbor, Maine; A.B., Dartmouth College, 1930; honorary M.A., Dartmouth College, 1942; LL.D., Fordham University, 1941; LL.D., Jewish Theological Seminary of America, 1950; director, Rockefeller Center, 1931-   ; president, 1938-45, 1948-51; chairman, 1945-53, 1956-58; director, Creole Petroleum Corporation, 1935-40; coordinator of Inter-American Affairs, 1940-44; assistant secretary of state, 1944-45; chairman, international development advisory board, Point Four Program, 1950-51; undersecretary of Health, Education and Welfare, 1953-54; special assistant to President, 1954-55; elected Republican governor, New York, 1958; reelected, 1962; officer, Museum of Modern Art; Metropolitan Museum of Art; Rockefeller Brothers Fund, Inc.; American International Association for Economic and Social Development; International Basic Economy Corporation; Phi Beta Kappa; recipient of Chile's Order of Merit, 1945; Brazilian National Order of the Southern Cross, 1946; Mexican Order of the Aztec Eagle, 1949; recipient of citations from National Conference of Christians and Jews, 1948, 1950; author, *The Future of Federalism,* 1962.   (See also *Current Biography: 1951.*)

SARNOFF, ROBERT W. (1918-   ). Born, New York City; graduate, Phillips Andover Academy, 1935; A.B., Harvard Uni-

versity, 1939, with major in government and philosophy; studied
law, Columbia University; LL.D., Pennsylvania Military College; Franklin and Marshall College; L.H.D., Boston University;
served in Office of Coordinator of Information, 1944; communications officer, United States Naval Reserve, 1942-45; served with
Cowles publications and broadcasting enterprises, 1945-48: in
Des Moines, Iowa, with *Register* and *Tribune,* later in New York
City with *Look* magazine; joined National Broadcasting Company,
1948; vice president, 1951-53; executive vice president, 1953-55;
director, 1953- ; president, 1955-58; chairman of board, 1958- ;
importantly associated with development of color television;
trustee, Franklin and Marshall College; Jewish Theological Seminary of America; recipient, Keynote award, National Association of Broadcasters, 1959; president, Radio and Television Executives Society, 1952-53; director, American Arbitration Association.
(See also *Current Biography: 1956.*)

SCRANTON, WILLIAM W. (1917-). Born, Madison, Connecticut; A.B., Yale University, 1939; LL.B., Yale University Law
School, 1946; admitted to Pennsylvania bar, 1946; captain, United
States Army Air Force, 1941-45; associated with and one-time
vice president of International Textbook Company and Haddon
Craftsmen, Inc., 1947-52; president, Scranton-Lackawanna Trust
Company, 1954-56; chairman of board, Northeastern Pennsyl-
vania Broadcasting Company, 1953-59; special assistant to Sec-
retary of State Christian A. Herter, 1959; member, United States
House of Representatives (Republican, Pennsylvania), 1961-62;
elected governor of Pennsylvania, 1962; vice president, Scranton
Chamber of Commerce, 1950-56; member of board, Keystone
College, 1952- ; International Textbook Company, 1949-60;
International Salt Company, 1955-60; Lackawanna Railroad,
1955-58; Geisinger Memorial Hospital and Foss Clinic, 1954- .

STEVENSON, ADLAI E. (1900-). Born, Los Angeles, California; attended public schools in Bloomington, Illinois, high school
of Illinois State Normal University, and Choate School; A.B.
Princeton University; LL.D., 1954; J.D., Northwestern University,
1926; LL.D., 1949; many other honorary degrees; admitted to

Illinois bar, 1926; practiced in Chicago, 1927-33; partner in law firm, 1935-41; assistant to secretary of navy, 1941-44; chief, economic mission to Italy, 1943; assistant to secretary of state, 1945; adviser, United States delegation, Conference on International Organization in San Francisco, 1945; chief, United States delegation, Preparatory Commission of the United Nations, London, 1945; United States delegate to General Assembly, 1946, 1947; governor of Illinois, 1949-53; Democratic candidate for President of the United States, 1952, 1956; with law firm, Chicago, 1955, 1957-60; United States representative to the United Nations, 1960- ; Distinguished Service Award, United States Navy, 1956; author, *Call to Greatness,* 1954; *What I Think,* 1956; *The New America,* 1957; *Friends and Enemies: What I Learned in Russia,* 1958; *Putting First Things First,* 1960; and others. (See also *Current Biography: 1961.*)

UNTEREINER, RAY E. (1898-). Born, Redlands, California; A.B., University of Redlands, 1920; A.M., Harvard University, 1921; Harvard University Law School, 1921-23; J.D., Mayo College of Law, Chicago, 1925; Ph.D., Northwestern University, 1932; instructor of economics, Harvard University, 1921-23; professor of speech and director of debate, Huron College, 1923-24; joined the staff of the California Institute of Technology in 1925; dean of freshmen students, 1937-43; professor of history and economics, 1943- ; visiting research professor, University of Hawaii, September 1961-January 1962; economist, National Association of Manufacturers, 1943-45; practiced law in California; consultant, Atomic Energy Commission, 1959-1961; member, Pasadena Board of Education, 1951-54; president, 1953-54; member, California Public Utilities Commission, 1954-58; chairman, committee on nuclear energy, National Association of Railroad and Utilities Commissioners, 1957-58; member, policy committee, Republican Central Committee of Los Angeles County; International Platform Association; Conference of Business Economists; author, *The Tax Racket: What We Pay To Be Governed,* 1933; contributor to journals.

WARREN, EARL (1891-   ). Born, Los Angeles, California; B.L., University of California, 1912; J.D., 1914; honorary degrees from College of the Pacific, University of Redlands, University of Southern California, Jewish Theological Seminary of America, and other institutions; admitted to California bar, 1914; deputy city attorney, Oakland, California, 1919-20; deputy district attorney, Alameda County, 1920-23; chief deputy district attorney, 1923-25; district attorney, 1925-39; held posts with Republican State Central Committee of California; attorney general of California, 1939-43; governor of California, 1943-53 (first governor to serve three terms); Republican candidate for Vice President of the United States, 1948; Chief Justice of the United States, 1953-   ; first lieutenant, United States Army, 1917-18; research associate, Bureau of Public Administration, University of California, 1932-40; chancellor, board of regents, Smithsonian Institution, 1953-   ; chairman, board of trustees, National Gallery of Art, 1953-   ; president, District Attorneys' Association of California, 1931-32; president, National Association of Attorneys General, 1940-41; trustee, American Philosophical Society. (See also *Current Biography: 1954.*)

CUMULATIVE AUTHOR INDEX
1960-1961—1962-1963

A cumulative author index to the volumes of REPRESENTATIVE AMERICAN SPEECHES for the years 1937-1938 through 1959-1960 appears in the 1959-1960 volume.